PLAY TO WIN
SQUASH

PLAY TO WIN

SQUASH

MALCOLM WILLSTROP

FOREWORD BY JONAH BARRINGTON

PEERAGE BOOKS

First published in 1987 by
Octopus Books Limited
59 Grosvenor Street
London W1

ISBN 0-7064-2889-7

Design by Laurence Bradbury Design Associates
Assisted by Sarah Collins

Colour artwork by Mulkern Rutherford Studio
Line illustrations by Klim Forster
Cartoon by Anni Axworthy

Art editor: Jeremy Bratt
Project editor: Tessa Rose
Copy-editor: Diana Vowles
Production: Peter Thompson

Typeset by SX Composing, Rayleigh, Essex
Colour origination by Mandarin, Hong Kong
Printed in Hong Kong

All photographs, except for the cover, were taken by
Stephen Line

CONTENTS

FOREWORD/6

INTRODUCTION/8

1 *SHOT-BY-SHOT : TECHNIQUES*/10

2 *SHOT ROUTINES*/26

3 *PRACTICE GAMES*/38

4 *GETTING IN SHAPE*/44

5 *MATCH PREPARATION*/48

6 *COURT CRAFT*/52

7 *TROUBLESHOOTING YOUR FAULTS*/60

8 *THE MIND AT PLAY*/66

9 *LEARNING BY WATCHING*/72

AFTERTHOUGHTS/78

INDEX/79

FOREWORD

Malcolm Willstrop is very much his own man and his approach to the teaching of the game of squash has always had a unique flavour. There are coaches who are reluctant to express an original viewpoint for fear of causing offence or being the object of ridicule, but Malcolm has always displayed that sound quality, strong opinion.

He is unquestionably the best teacher of squash technique to youngsters, both boys and girls, and has greatly emphasized the need for good footwork and general relaxation in play. He has coached extensively at all levels, and whether one is watching his club players, his young stars – Cassie Jackman and David Campion – or the proven professional – Gawain Briars – it is abundantly clear that his method is certain and perpetuated through his fortunate pupils.

Malcolm's book on squash has been long-awaited and will be avidly read and studied – not only by those who have sat at his feet, but perhaps more importantly by the many thousands of squash enthusiasts who will never have had the opportunity of being taught by him. *Play to Win: Squash* provides us with a comprehensive catalogue of advice and, indeed, reassurance. The drawings and diagrams – always so important – have been well prepared and blend perfectly with the text. One can write about the essentials of good footwork and balance, but the reader – sometimes in doubt – will have his fears stilled as he studies the stars depicting the very essence of Malcolm's squash philosophy. At the same time we are shown how not to do it – a gentle reminder to those who are set in their ways that it is not necessarily the end of the world!

I have long admired Malcolm Willstrop's independence of mind and his generosity of spirit. A powerful motivator, he is one of the few great teachers of our time; a man whose qualities fit him for the central role of squash guide to the young, eager and ambitious. *Play to Win: Squash* should be an integral part of every squash enthusiast's life and library.

Jonah Barrington

Jonah Barrington, enjoying his dominance of Ahmed Safwat, moves in for the kill.

INTRODUCTION

HOW TO IMPROVE

A large part of the pleasure derived from playing squash is the action itself; action which involves movement, the rewarding feeling of hitting a ball off the middle of the racket (even if only occasionally!), the noise the ball makes on the wall when it has been well struck. And afterwards there is the glow that comes only from physical exertion, that feeling of wellbeing as the body basks, relaxed and contented. There are some players who even derive their pleasure from port-mortems in the changing room. Maybe this will satisfy some, but there is equal satisfaction to be had from improving your standard or at least reaching a standard in accordance with your ability. Rather there may be dissatisfaction on reaching a state where no further improvement is forthcoming! Older players may put down stagnation to advancing years, mistaken conception though this is, since it is much more attitude of mind which affects the possibility of improving or not. Lack of ability may be a better explanation, but few players will recognize that!

One of the many advantages of squash for the beginner is that it is not too difficult for most people to hit the ball against the wall. The hitting of a ball over a net, as in tennis, causes more of a problem. You don't need to be especially gifted to get started, though obviously the more natural ability you have, the quicker will be your rate of improvement. In truth, it does not take long to hit the ball well enough to develop some sort of rally. Nor do you need to be particularly athletic, unless you want to make quick progress.

If you are a beginner, the best thing you can do is to seek guidance so that you learn correct technique early on. As with any form of learning, progress will be surer and more rapid if it is well based, and there is no doubt that squash requires a well-defined technique. It is much more difficult to remedy faults once they become established and if guidance is not sought initially, it is probable that any potential you have will not be fully realized. So, pay particular attention to the chapters on technique and the suggested routines that accompany each shot.

But whether you are a beginner or an old hand, what makes a difference to your standard of play is the number of times you get on court; the quality and variety of your playing partners; your opportunities for beneficial match play; whether you practise as opposed to play games, and your physical condition.

Any player who bemoans his lack of improvement may, on closer inspection, be found to be playing the same opponent(s) on a regular basis so that he or she is familiar with every move and no longer needs original thought. To improve, players require stimulus and that comes from the variety to be had from playing many different opponents. Internal league and club matches will provide this. If you are not involved in either form of match play, you must seek your own opponents.

Of course, no player will improve unless he is playing sufficiently, since one of the most relevant factors in a racket sport is the number of balls you hit correctly. But if you are playing say two or three times a week then what you do on those occasions is very important. What most average players, who may well be capable of considerable improvement, rarely do is practise: they moan about their inability to play a drop shot and they cannot lob, but they don't practise either shot! No-one has a divine right to make difficult shots. Some players may have a natural talent, which still needs properly utilizing, while others will have to work at it from the start. If you fall in the latter category, don't worry, for lack of natural talent need not be such a disadvantage ultimately.

My advice to any player is to spend a proportion of his or her time practising rather than simply playing games. Good advice this may be, but the practicalities of it may be more difficult, since it requires like-minded players with whom to practise and it is clear that they are few and far between.

Since systematic practice is relatively unusual for the average player, you will need to know how to do it, which shots to concentrate on, the technique involved and the precise requirements of any practice you undertake. This is where *Play to Win: Squash* will help you, for set down here are descriptions of most of the principal shots and the technique

Bryan Beeson in full cry, moving forward on the forehand.

required to play them successfully, followed by practices which bring the shots into play, either singly or collectively. It provides a basis for the player who wants to know how to set about practising, and therefore improving. Working from this basis, in co-operation with a partner of similar intent, you should quickly make headway. If all the suggested shots are regularly practised, they should give you an all-round command of the court, increasing your confidence and your options.

If you represent the average player, in a rut, but not satisfied with your playing standard, now's the time to change your routine and add practice to your playing. Practices, especially the more demanding ones, have the considerable advantage of improving not only your skills, but also your fitness for the game. When skills and fitness are brought along together, then maximum benefit is being derived from the time you spend on court – and that is the key to improvement.

SHOT-BY-SHOT : TECHNIQUES

THE GRIP/STRAIGHT HITTING

All the shots I shall deal with are vital to give you range and options. Obviously, no-one will be equally good at them all, but your weaker shots can be improved by regular practice. Each shot discussed in this chapter is cross-referenced to an appropriate practice routine to help you improve any shot that you consider weak. It is ironic that some players do not like practising a certain shot because they are no good at it – this is not a fruitful philosophy! Remember too that while it is a good idea to remedy those niggling weaknesses in your armoury, it shouldn't be at the expense of your strengths, which will rapidly lose their potency if you neglect them. In the words of the Chinese proverb: 'What you don't use you lose'.

To put in a lot of hard work requires not only time but the inclination, for not everybody wants to be dedicated even to a minor extent. There is nothing wrong with that – it's up to you to work out what you want for yourself.

If you are a beginner, you should spend much of your time in the initial stages practising hitting the ball correctly – you will have to wait for a while before you tackle a game.

The first strokes you are likely to make are cross-court shots which are returned to your practice partner or coach. At this stage they are played to improve the swing and movement, but later you will see that they take on much greater significance.

However, it is almost certain that the first shot you will practise will be hitting straight down the side wall. You'll soon see that being able to hit the ball accurately and consistently close to the side wall is a vital requirement, as it is one of the shots which provides a platform from which to play and subsequently attack. We'll begin with this basic aim, but first we'll look at the grip.

The grip

The grip is an important factor in the proper execution of all of the strokes. Hold the shaft of the racket in your left hand and take hold of the handle with the right, as if you are shaking hands. The fingers should then be wrapped round the handle, but not clenched.

A 'V' will now have formed between your thumb and forefinger. The thumb should not run loosely along the top of the handle, but should curl round to meet the fingers. The heel of the hand should rest at the base of the grip.

You will see players with unorthodox grips and they may be excellent performers, but you will still be better served by having an orthodox grip from the beginning.

Straight hitting

This shot is played mostly from the front of the court. The best position to adopt in this area is a front foot lead – if you are right-handed, the left foot on the forehand and right foot on the backhand. This will ensure a forward inclination of your body towards the ball, which in its turn will ensure that your body and racket are moving in harmony (see illustration below). It also means that your head will be well over the ball and that your eyes are therefore more likely to be on the ball.

It is important to be the right distance from the ball and for a beginner, especially if you are unfamiliar with racket games, this may often prove a difficulty at first. The correct distance is when your arm and racket are

To hit the ball straight and accurately, your body and racket must be in harmony, hence the forward inclination. The ball should be closely watched, too. The swing shown here is close to the point of contact.

Phil Kenyon in perfect position
on the forehand.

STRAIGHT/CROSS COURT HITS

comfortably extended towards the ball. You will easily establish whether you are too close to the ball as you will probably miss it altogether, mishit it or if you do hit it the position will feel restricted and uncomfortable.

The most advantageous time to strike the ball is when it is marginally in front of your leading foot. Once the ball passes this point there will be limitations on the stroke, especially on the backhand side where, once past the front foot, the ball is past the racket.

Now you have established the correct position, let's consider the racket. You should prepare the racket early with your wrist firm and cocked and the racket head high. The swing should be full, rhythmical, smooth and relaxed, all of which will aid control as well as conserve energy. It sounds simple enough, but you may not find it so to achieve!

If your racket meets the ball at the wrong point, the ball will either come back across your body towards the centre of the court or hit the side wall first. In the first instance the racket has gone through the ball too early and in the second instance, too late. If the racket is too early, the leading shoulder may often have opened up too much – a common fault.

If you are hitting the ball straight down the wall from deeper in the court, it will usually be more difficult to lead with the front foot and you can transfer more weight to the back foot. However, adopt a position as sideways to the front wall as you are able in order to keep the ball straight. Where possible, if time allows, it is still preferable to lead with the front foot.

Once you have established this technique your goal is to be precise in the placement of the ball. Closeness to the wall should always be your aim and any straight ball should not hit the side wall but run directly into the back corners. The lower the ball is struck the more pressure it will put on your opponent.

Routines and games
- Straight hitting, page 26
- Straight hit with angle: with movement, page 29
- Double feed 1, page 35
- Going solo 1, page 37
- Straight v normal, page 41

Cross court hitting
When you are playing a match, cross court hitting is very important, and one of the pillars of a good game. If you are in a position of attack at the front of the court, balls will be easily intercepted and punished if they are struck through the middle of the court, thus turning an opportunity for attack into pressured defence.

It is crucial, then, that you are aware of the need to hit the ball wide and preferably low. The line along which the ball should travel will mean that it will make contact with the side wall about 46cm (18 inches) behind the service box. Your opponent, however well placed in the centre of the court, will thus not be able to intercept. Hitting the ball low will increase the difficulty for an opponent, since even if the cross court line is not perfect, it will be harder for him or her to pick up and deal effectively with a low ball. The worst type of cross court ball (ie, the one your opponent will think the best and will eagerly punish) is about shoulder high through the middle of the court.

It is also important that the cross court ball is not 'short'; that is, reaching the side wall too early. What invariably happens in this instance is that the ball bounces off the side wall and comes out towards the centrally placed opponent, who will find such a ball all too easy to deal with.

Front foot leads again provide the best positions from which to play cross court at the front of the court. You will often find it necessary to play the ball further ahead of the front foot than when hitting straight. Playing accurately cross court from the back of the court is by no means easy, as you will tend to hit the ball higher than is desirable, making it vulnerable to interception.

Since the cross court shot so readily transfers initiative in a rally, you must above all be aware of the need to keep the ball wide and low. That awareness, coupled with regular practice, will bring about improvement if the cross court is a weak part of your game. Watch a match with particular attention to cross court play and you will see the undesirable effects poorly hit cross court shots may have for the perpetrator.

Qamar Zaman under pressure
on the forehand volley, but he
retains his balance and
control of the racket.

VOLLEY

While not subscribing to the widely publicized view that Pakistanis have superhuman squash abilities – Jahangir Khan may be an exception! – they have always impressed me as the best cross court players. Their game has in it a strong element of cross court play and it is clearly an area of the game they have practised and perfected.

Routines and games
- Cross court hit and angle, page 28
- Straight drop and angle – straight hit and cross court hit, page 32
- Angles and cross courts, page 42

Volley

Although the volley is by no means an easy shot for the beginner, it has to appear in your repertoire quite early, since returning serve may often depend on the ability to volley – and serving itself is a form of volley, requiring similar timing and co-ordination.

Any weakness in your control of the racket head caused by lack of firmness in your wrist

The volley exposes any deficiencies in racket head control. The main points to remember are that the stance should be more upright and that the racket head should be well up. Good balance remains an essential requirement.

FOREHAND FAVOURITES

"The forehand volley and the forehand drop are my two favourite shots. I like to aim the volley for the straight nick, and I always try to get into a balanced position for the drop." – *Liz Irving*

will quickly be shown up in the volley. You must hold the racket firmly and make every effort to get the racket through the ball with as full face as possible. Although there is automatic cut on the backhand volley with the racket face travelling across the line of the ball, any exaggeration will very probably lead to mistiming and error. It should be possible to volley on the forehand with almost the full face of the racket, though once again there is a natural, if marginal, opening of the racket face (see illustration below left).

Getting too close to the ball is a major source of error when volleying and when you play this shot you should aim to stretch comfortably into the ball.

Even when you have mastered the volley technically, there are different problems associated with volleys of varying height and direction.

The high volley above the head – off lobs, for instance – may often cause you to hit into the tin, for in your anxiety to attack the ball you will quicken up the stroke and snatch at the ball, thus hitting through it too early. The tin becomes the obvious attraction. Another problem is that when the ball is high in the air it is too easy not to watch it closely enough. Watching the ball is fundamental to your game and high balls need extra care (see illustration on page 64).

Low volleys are another difficult area and a frequent source of error when players fail to get down to the ball. Tall players are considered to be especially susceptible to the low volley, but that may only be if they are not especially aware of the problem or if they are not flexible enough in their movement. Often the low volley may be played when the ball is dropping from the highest point of its trajectory and that, too, will create difficulties.

Another volley which you will find awkward is when the ball is coming at you directly, often very fast. This arises frequently when the ball is hit, albeit inaccurately, down the middle of the court at the unsuspecting player. What is then vital is your ability to manipulate the racket quickly, something at which not everyone is adept. It also helps if, not having time to adjust your feet, you can bend your upper body to make room to use the racket. Remaining in an upright position will not help.

The ability to volley affects return of service, one of the most crucial shots in squash, so any practice you do to improve your volley is time well spent.

Routines and games

- Continuous straight feed for volley, page 28
- Double feed 2, page 36
- Co-operative cross court volleying from mid court line, page 33
- Co-operative cross court volleying from deeper in the court, page 34
- Going solo 2, page 37
- Going solo 3, page 37
- One for the volley, page 40
- Above the cut line, page 42

Angles

Although the terms 'angle' and 'boast' are both used to describe the ball which hits the side wall before reaching the front wall, 'angle' is used in this book to refer to all such shots, whether they be at the front of the court or the back.

In the same way that the volley has to come early in your development, so must the angle played from deep positions in the court, since this is the shot that gives you a chance to survive a ball that has passed you and reached the back of the court.

The shot demands correct positioning and if you get this wrong it will be reflected in the result. It is a shot that is all too often played incorrectly, even by high class performers.

The best way to tackle it is to lead into the ball off the front foot, facing the side wall, the direction in which you are going to hit the ball (see illustrations below). You must hit the ball firmly, otherwise it will probably not reach the front wall. It must hit the side wall some 60cm (2ft) or so in front of the leading foot. If you hit the ball too directly at the side wall it will not reach the front wall; if it hits the side wall too far in front of your feet it will hit the front wall

Below left: To hit the forehand angle from deeper positions, take up a stance facing the side wall. Keep well over the ball and away from the side wall to allow yourself room for a full swing.

Below right: For the deep backhand angle the feet should be facing the side wall and pointing in the direction that the ball is to be struck. The racket head should be kept well up, and remain so during the follow through.

ANGLES

too early and come out to the centre of the court. Both these failings are very common and you need to understand how they occur, so you can rectify them. Once you have mastered the shot you should make every effort to keep the ball low on the front wall, since high angles, no matter how accurate, are very vulnerable. To achieve this, you must hit the ball low into the side wall.

The angle from the back of the court is essentially defensive, but, well played, can turn defence into attack and at the highest levels can be an outright winner when it finds the nick.

The further up the playing scale you go the more likely you will be to avoid the defensive angle, since it is generally safer to hit the ball straight and by the time you reach higher levels you will have acquired the considerable art of being able to straighten the ball out from difficult positions. Apocryphal or not, Geoff Hunt, one of the world's greatest players, is reputed to be responsible for the remark, 'Consider carefully playing an angle, then don't!'

It is probably true that in the past, reared on cold courts and without the high levels of physical fitness that are now called for, more players used angles as part of their game. It is equally true that today's players, used to warmer playing conditions which cause angles to sit up more, play them much less often – although there have been a few top-class players who had a particular skill with the angle. Ahmed Safwat and Gogi Alauddin are two that spring to mind and it is worth noting that both were craftsmen of a high order and eminently watchable at the same time. The variety created by use of angles is, among other things, what made them so good to watch.

If your opponent is slow moving or when he tires, the angle played from anywhere in the court can become an attacking force. What you need then is an awareness of the moment to introduce the angle and the practical ability to produce it at a particular time in a match, having perhaps not previously used it to any great extent.

Unlike the deeper angle, the short angle, played at the front of the court, is an attacking shot. Again it is best played off the front foot, since in this way it is easier to disguise your intentions. Disguise is a crucial element in the shot, since if it is delayed and hidden it will be doubly effective (see illustrations below).

Below left: Positioning for the forehand short angle is often difficult. The position shown here will not only help you play the shot but will disguise your intention from your opponent, since it will be easy for you to shield the ball with your body.

Below right: The short backhand angle played from the front of the court. You should get over the ball and keep the racket head up as you strike through the ball and into the follow through.

Ahmed Safwat lines up one of the angles for which he is famous.

SHOT-BY-SHOT: TECHNIQUES

ANGLES/SERVICE

Your positioning in playing the short angle is very important; common faults are closeness to the ball, thus inhibiting the racket, and running through the ball with the back foot, so that you end up against the wall and badly out of position. Running through the ball may also lead to error and will certainly remove any element of surprise the shot may have. It is, of course, absolutely vital that your feet are still and you are well balanced when any shot is played (see page 60).

On the forehand side, it is not unusual for the shot to be played from a position square to the front wall. Without recommending this, it does enhance the disguise for some players. Providing it is played with awareness and is effective, it is perfectly allowable. It is one of those improvised shots which are built from a sound, well-established basic technique (see illustration below).

The racket has to be well controlled as the shot demands a high degree of skill and if your wrist, and therefore the racket head, drops, there is a high risk of error. The dropping of the racket head is a common fault here (see page 62).

The short angle, well played and produced at opportune moments, has much to recom-mend it and it may well be true that it is too sparsely used, especially at high levels. The reason for that, though, is clear, since if it is badly played it can be disastrous.

Angles of all kinds are better executed on the backhand, principally because positioning is usually more correct on that side.

Routines and games
- Cross court lob and angle, page 28
- Second routine in straight hitting, page 26
- Two angles, page 33
- Straight volley feed and volleyed angle from mid court line, page 29
- Angles and cross courts, page 42
- Angles only, page 42

Service
Since it comes at the beginning of the rally, the service may well influence the whole course of subsequent play for the point, so you should not underestimate it. It is all too easy to do this because it does not have the obvious effect that it does, say, in tennis.

While the service is important to all players at all times, it has special significance at the extreme playing levels of the game. A begin-ner may well have trouble volleying; will cer-tainly have trouble volleying after the ball has made contact with the side wall, and will be severely tested by any ball that gets into the back corners. To serve well as a beginner, therefore, will very often put fellow beginners into difficulty. There is, though, a danger that too much reliance can thus be placed on the serve at the cost of general play. While begin-ners should learn to serve well, they should not become obsessed by it!

Advanced players, too, must take care with the serve since their equally skilled opponents will readily punish any weakness. If the service is directly onto the volley of the receiver, he or she may well be good enough to hit it 'dead'. At worst the weak serve will probably be re-turned in such a way as to exert pressure from the beginning of the rally, pressure a pro-ficient player is unlikely to relax.

Although many varying and sometimes un-usual forms of serve may be seen in any club, it is best to develop a technique which lends

The squarer stance necessary for playing the forehand reverse angle; it should open up in the direction in which the ball will be struck.

Ross Thorne gets the ball well on its way as he projects the serve.

itself to reliability and consistency.

On both sides of the court, place the right foot inside and the left foot outside the service box. On the backhand side this will give a balanced position and on the forehand side it will open up your position in the direction you need to project the ball. (See illustrations on page 20.)

The foot inside the box should be as close to the inner red line as possible so that you are as near to the centre of the court as the rule allows – the centre being the position you will take, having served. The centre of the court is a good pace behind the 'T', so it is practical to assume a central position for the serve.

It is often difficult for a beginner to time the

SERVICE

Right: When serving from the forehand side the left foot should be well outside the service box to make it easier for you to project the ball at the correct angle on to the front wall.

Far right: The position for the serve on the backhand side shows the left foot outside the box and the right foot just inside. A good stretch out of the box will put you nearer the centre of the court.

throwing up of the ball with the swing, but with practice and reasonable co-ordination this can soon be improved. Once you have mastered the action of the service you can concentrate more on direction. Advanced players have no problem with the mechanics of the service and can direct all their effort towards accuracy and variety.

What all players need is a basic serve which is dependable, offers little risk of going out – to serve out is hardly excusable – and in general makes contact with the side wall relatively deep in the court, making the volley difficult. A good serve will force the opponent back and often commit the receiver to an angle.

Once you have established a basic serve, you can develop variations: the harder hit, lower trajectory serve aimed well to the back of the service box; the hard hit serve directly at the receiver; and a higher lobbed serve with much less pace are some possibilities.

There are many players who produce backhand serves especially from the forehand side, but they are often low in trajectory and

vulnerable. The advantage of serving backhand from the forehand side, besides a change of angle, is that the receiver is in full view of the server all the time.

When players are in the beginner category they will invariably serve to what they perceive to be their opponent's weakness, the backhand, forgetting that the backhand, like all shots, will improve with use and as the player grows in experience. To serve automatically to the backhand is not advisable. It is wise to take stock of your opponent's imbalance of strengths and weaknesses on a particular side of the court and act accordingly.

The days when cold courts encouraged the development of the serve are long gone – and that may be as well, for a dominant serve on cold courts did little to encourage the development of rallies; but beware of the lackadaisical serve, the main purpose of which seems to be just to put the ball in play.

Routines and games
● Returning the serve straight : play down the side walls, page 42

Far left: When you prepare to receive, take up a position sideways to the front wall and ensure that the racket head is up in a state of readiness. Watch the ball from the server's hand.

Left: The same principles apply when you are receiving serve on the backhand side: a sideways position, well prepared racket and eyes towards the server. The stance should be easy and relaxed.

Return of service

Just as the serve may determine the subsequent action of any rally, the return of serve may have even more effect.

It is safe to say that, where possible, volleying the serve is your best course of action. If you have enough confidence in your volley, it will prevent you from having to play out of the troublesome back corners. An advanced player will use it to get onto the attack, giving his or her opponent less time to re-organize after serving.

You should aim to volley the return straight and providing you can play the ball close to the wall the height and pace of the volley is less important. Volleying straight is no easy skill, however, and to get the ball straight, the best positions are sideways on. If you adopt a square-on position it is quite likely the ball will be pulled across court towards the middle (see illustrations above).

A high, wide volley return cross court is a perfectly acceptable shot and if the service is difficult, this may be an alternative. It is crucial that you put the ball high and wide, otherwise your opponent may easily intercept it.

If the server presents a simple volley conveniently on to your racket, then there are all manner of attacking possibilities: hitting the ball into the cross court nick; drop volleys; and hard hit straight winners, but these shots require a high level of skill!

Returning the serve after it has hit the side wall is a difficult shot, but it will improve with practice. Many players fail to give ground away from the wall, and so end up playing too close to the ball.

The deep angle is the last line of defence, unless you choose to play it for some specific reason; and since angles will invariably leave you in a defensive situation, it is vital that you play them well – that is, low and wide.

When you are receiving serve, what you need to be able to do most of all is to make the

DROPS

right selection. You must choose the right moment to go in and volley directly, the correct moment to wait, to volley off the wall, or to play the angle. You will have to make your choices quickly and you will pay dearly for any indecision.

Selecting the best return of service is no simple matter, but with practice and experience you will soon see results.

Routines and games
- Returning the serve straight: play down the side walls, page 42
- Play with the ball having to land within either rectangle, page 43

Drops
Most of the shots you've read about so far have involved hitting the ball hard, though of course volleys can be played with touch and angles can be played with delicacy.

The drop, however, is concerned only with touch. The purpose of this shot is to bring your opponent into the front of the court to manoeuvre him or her out of position, to catch your opponent off guard at the back of the court and in general to change the pace and break up the established pattern of play.

The colder the court the more necessary it becomes for you to have a drop shot as part of your repertoire. In days gone by, players

DEFT DROPS

"My two favourite shots are the backhand drop from the front of the court and from deeper. I like to play them in quite decisively with the required amount of cut." – *Susan Devoy*

who learned the game exclusively on cold courts were adept at the drop shot. As the game of squash has developed, playing conditions have become warmer and improved standards of fitness have meant that drop shots are more consistently picked up; players new to the game have understandably been less aware of this shot. Nor has the obsession with non-marking green balls done much to encourage the subtleties of the drop, since no matter how delicate the touch or skilful the player the green ball will bounce up, making itself available to the superfit chaser. Those who have sanctioned the green balls have much to answer for in terms of making the game a less attractive spectacle. Nevertheless, although playing circumstances may have altered the drop shot remains an essential part of your armoury.

You may play the drop shot from any part of the court your skill allows, but your first inclination should be to think of it as a shot

Below left: To play the drop well at the front of the court, you must get down low in the same way that you would for the lob, but the racket face will not generally be as open. Maintain your balance and you'll find recovery far easier.

Below right: For the backhand drop the racket face should be open and the wrist cocked to keep the racket head up. The extent to which you have to get down will depend on the height of the ball off the floor.

Far left: The deep forehand drop is a difficult shot and one that few play well. Good positioning is crucial: play the shot sideways to the front wall and ensure that your wrist is up.

Left: Good balance is necessary for playing a backhand drop from deep in court. The body should be inclined forwards, despite the deep position, and the racket head should be well up.

played from the front of the court.

Your position is vital, as the drop shot is often played off relatively low balls and you must bend to get well down and over the ball. Playing too upright, especially if you are tall, will invariably lose you the point. Here again, front foot positions are better than square or back foot positions since they enable you to get down more easily and in a more balanced manner.

The drop at the front of the court can be played to win the rally outright. Play it at an angle towards the nick with the intention of making the ball unplayable or play it straight, delicately, to run close to the side wall and stay close to the front wall. This drop shot can also be used to manoeuvre your opponent, making it difficult for him or her to make a worthwhile return, rather than to win the rally outright. Though if the drop is executed as well as is possible, it may well do exactly that!

As well as getting your position right, your control of the racket head with such a subtle shot is of paramount importance, which may explain why not everyone finds it easy to master. Ideally the racket head should be high and must be firmly controlled from the wrist. On the forehand side the face of the racket

should be slightly open (see illustration on page 22). The pace of the racket through the ball will determine the quality of the shot.

The backhand drop is played with more cut – that is, when the racket face travels across the line of ball – though there is the obvious danger of error if you overdo the cutting action or open up the racket face too much (see illustration on page 22).

The majority of players are more successful with the backhand rather than the forehand drop and there are few more expert at that shot played at the front or back of the court than Susan Devoy, the Ladies World Champion; see photograph on page 25.

Playing drop shots from deeper in the court, usually in the three quarter court area off opponents' shots which have failed to penetrate, requires skill reinforced by a lot of practice. This shot is more frequently, and better, played on the backhand side, because players find it much more difficult to take up the correct position on the forehand side. (See illustrations above.)

Just as at the front, the deeper shot can be played straight to find the wall or into the nick, and certainly the angle from which the ball is played will encourage you to aim for the nick.

SHOT-BY-SHOT : TECHNIQUES

DROPS/LOB

The lob demands that you get down very low to lift the ball. The racket face must open to assist elevation. The pace should be off the ball, so lightness of touch is required.

Both the deeper drops are played naturally with more cut than the front drops, though the forehand deep drop can be just as effective played with a fuller-faced racket, if you have the necessary touch – and not everyone has.

You need to develop tactical awareness of when to execute the drop shot and part of that awareness will be an appreciation of the playing conditions which will affect it. However, you would not be wise to eliminate drop shots just because conditions are warm and the ball bouncy. Your aim should always be to manoeuvre the ball and vary the pace.

The right moment to execute the front court drop will often be obvious, but don't fall into the trap of trading drops when a simple hit to the back of the court would complete the rally. It stands to reason that having brought your opponent forward the next thing is to move him or her to the back – a simple conception, but one that it is easy to lose sight of in the heat of battle.

Choosing the moment to play the drop from deeper in the court probably requires more cunning since your opponent will be in front of you and therefore nearer to where the ball will end up. Be aware of the balance of your opponent. Is he in a position to move forward easily? Is he a good mover to the front of the court? Is he watching behind well enough?

The cross court drop is a variation based on the straight drop. Once your opponent is looking for the straight drop, that is the time to insert the cross court alternative. From then on the doubt is always there, leaving your opponent feeling less secure (always supposing, of course, that the shots are well played!)

You can play the cross court drop from the front of the court or from deeper in the same way as the straight drop, but you will use it far less frequently than the straight drop, especially from the back. This shot is played more often purely with the intent of winning the rally, more often than not directed into the cross court nick.

Not everyone finds the drop an easy shot to master, but you should put in some regular and sustained practice to make it part of your armoury of shots. You'll never be really complete without it!

Routines and games
- Two drops with movement, page 30
- Drop: counter drop with movement, page 31
- Double feeds 3 and 4, page 36
- Lob and drop, page 43

Lob
The lob is essentially a defensive shot, played under pressure to create time to recover your position – and because you are under pressure, it is not easy. Like the drop, the lob is often played off low balls, requiring you to get down and, in the instance of the lob, well under the ball (see illustration above). If you fail to do this or to open the racket face sufficiently, you will have problems getting enough height on the ball.

The height on the lob is crucial to clear the opponent, but the width is important too. Any lob that is lacking in height will be easy to punish and although lack of width is marginally less serious, it will not aid the lobber's cause. Players often lack the necessary touch and delicacy on the lob and their efforts are almost hits. The touch you need for the lob is similar to that required for the drop. Apart from giving you a chance to recover position, the lob has the added advantage of changing pace and if it is well executed it will convert

what is a defensive situation into an attacking one. Perfectly executed, it will produce an outright winner.

The lob, like the drop, works best in cooler conditions, but don't neglect it on warmer courts. It is principally a cross court shot but lobbing the ball straight is equally effective, though more difficult to master. If the cross court lob is under-used, then the straight lob or 'floater' is even more so.

Routines and games
- Cross court lob and angle/volleyed angle, page 28
- Straight lob and volley drop, page 32
- Lob and drop, page 43

Susan Devoy plays the backhand drop from deep in the court – no one does it better.

SHOT ROUTINES

STRAIGHT HITTING

There is no escape from the regular need to practise and, regardless of your ability, the greater the number of technically correct and well directed balls you hit the better. Proper practice will help you to fulfil your potential and even when you have reached your highest standard you will still have to practise to remain there.

There is little point in practising aimlessly; less time well spent is much better. Therein lies a serious problem for many players, even those of high standard and aspirations. You may not have an environment conducive to worthwhile practice. You probably will not have a coach or professional assistance; you may not have regular, like-minded practice partners, with whom you can work over a prolonged period; and nor may you have the co-operation of a club, which you will most definitely need if you are hoping to reach professional standards. To do this you will need access to courts – happily at convenient times of the day – without in any way being made to feel uncomfortable. How you are treated may well depend on what you give back to the club, both socially and in playing terms.

The fragmented way in which even leading squash players often have to practise will rarely bring about fulfilment of potential. There is no doubt that you can achieve the most given good practice partners and conditions, but these circumstances hardly exist and where they do, it is only on the basis of goodwill rather than in any official way. So to do well as a squash player, you may well have to succeed despite circumstances.

The more varied the practice you can manage the better, since variety will help maintain your interest and provide the necessary stimulus. You can achieve this variety by practising with different partners and by having as many routines as possible at hand – but no matter how many routines you may have, they will have to be repeated. There is no quick or easy way to improve your standard of play. Practice routines, however tiresome you may think them, are necessary. If repetition suggests boredom, the remedy is in your hands, not only to make your routines more interesting but, more importantly, to change your attitude towards them!

The shot routines suggested here are, of course, in no way comprehensive, but I have found them most effective over many years of coaching. They incorporate aspects of court craft as well as basic technical skills and are designed to help you build your game. You'll need a partner for most of them (for some you'll need two or more), but I have included several practices that can be performed solo.

Straight hitting: fed, then combined with drop shot

Hitting the ball straight, low and close to the side wall is a principal shot in squash and once you can hit the ball reasonably well you should practise this shot to perfect it.

This particular shot is important to players of all levels, since it provides a platform from which to play. The better you become the more precisely and accurately you will need to hit the ball.

To practise hitting straight, position yourself just in front of the mid-court line, slightly to the right of centre, and work towards the front wall to make the shot, recovering to the original position each time.

Your coach or playing partner is positioned at the back of the court as the feeder to set up the ball for you. As with all feeding, it has to be accurate and consistent, which should come readily to a coach, but may not always do so to a player!

In this instance the feed should be light, so that the ball does not come too far back in the court. Properly fed, the ball will be in such a position that you will have every chance to play it correctly. If the feed is too strong it will cause you to rush and also to play the ball late, that is, behind your feet. This will invariably make you mishit, most frequently the ball hitting the side walls first and coming out towards the middle.

Once you are at ease with this practice routine it can be made more valuable for both of you. Instead of the back court player acting as a feeder, he or she can now play as good a drop shot as possible off the straight hit. This is a much more difficult practice and it is not

The enigmatic Australian
Tristan Nancarrow attacks the
cross court nick.

SHOT ROUTINES

STRAIGHT FEEDS/CROSS COURTS

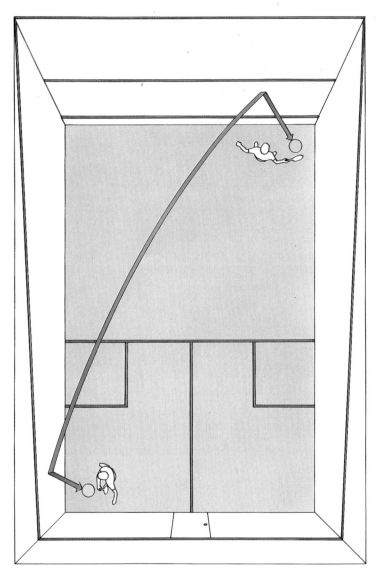

Diagram 1: **Cross court hit and angle. The front court player hits a cross court shot for his partner at the back to play an angle.**

worth trying if either of you is not capable of sustaining the drop shot.

It is important, as in all practices, that you play the shots as correctly as possible, since improvisation is not the purpose – correct technique is!

It is so vital to be able to hit the ball straight, low and precisely that any time you spend on this practice can never be wasted.

Continuous straight feed for the volley

Transferring from the first practice to this one is simple, since both players stay in the same areas of the court.

Your partner should make the feed from just behind the service box and set it up lightly. Too strong a feed from too far up the court would only put you under too much pressure. Ideally the ball should reach you at a comfortable volleying height.

Your targets when volleying remain much the same as when hitting the ball after the bounce; straight, close to the wall and low, though to get the ball low will be considerably more difficult than it is off the bounce.

This is not a particularly easy routine for the beginner, but it is valuable and will become much more straightforward with practice.

Cross court hit and angle

Here is another practice equally useful for both players, since neither shot is fed. The front court player's task is to hit the ball cross court, with the emphasis on hitting the ball low and very much on the right line, and the back court player, operating behind the service box, plays an angle back in the partner's direction. (See diagram 1.)

This is a combination of two important shots, both of which, if played badly in a match, will leave any player under extreme pressure.

Cross court lob and angle/volleyed angle

This is a variation on the previous practice. The front court player plays the cross court lob, wide, high and with the pace off the ball, and the back court player plays the angle, mostly volleyed, but with the option of playing it off the bounce.

Both these shots, especially the volleyed angle, require a high degree of skill and timing, so save this routine until you have reached a high standard of play!

Straight hit with angle – with movement

This is the first practice requiring a lot of movement on the part of both you and your partner. (See diagram 2.)

The front court player hits straight balls down both sides of the court, moving from side to side from a position well in front of the mid court line.

The back court player plays angles on both sides of the court, moving side to side from a position behind the service box.

Since the movement is side to side there is no great pressure and, as usual, try to move in a relaxed and easy manner.

Accuracy and precision of the two shots will make it harder for both players without disrupting the practice. Even quality players will not hit such a high percentage of precise shots that the practice will be too difficult.

This routine is often done in a slipshod and imprecise way, mainly because players will hit both shots too high on the wall. In this case it is not really worth the trouble.

Straight volley feed and volleyed angle from mid court line

This is a development from the previous practice, involving much more pressure both in movement and racket control.

The front court player, who will be well forward, is essentially a feeder, but there will still be pressure on movement and setting up the ball accurately and consistently will require control.

His or her job is to present the back court player, who works across the mid court line, with a volley off which to play an angle. The fed volley, therefore, should not be too high (somewhere between waist and shoulder height) and should be paced to help the back court player's movement and striking of the ball. Ideally, the volleyer will stretch comfortably into the ball. The rear player will play low angled volleys off the fed volleys.

Rhythm is a crucial part of the practice and

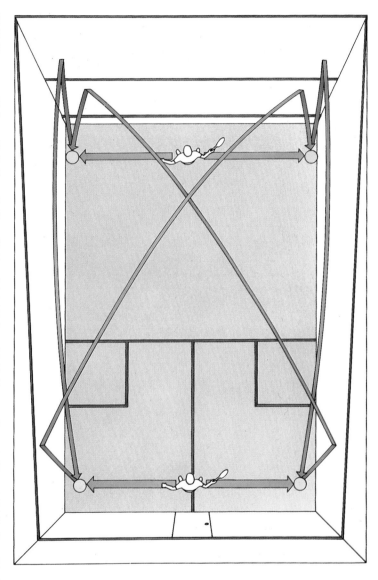

Diagram 2: Straight hit combined with angle with movement. The front court player hits straight shots down the side walls to his partner at the back who plays angles.

DROPS

you can increase the pace according to your ability and your partner's.

Two drop shots with movement
The front court player's role is purely that of a feeder, setting up a drop at the front of the court which will be countered by the back court player. The second feed will be a lobbed ball without pace into the service box, preferably towards the back. After playing the drop at the front, the player moves back into the service box to play a second, deeper drop. Repeat continuously.

It is important that you try to get behind the

Hiddy Jahan improvises with his footwork on the forehand.

COUNTER DROP

ball when playing the deeper drop because failure to do this will force you to improvise.

Drop: counter drop with movement

This practice uses the drop at the front of the court. The feeder sets up a continuous stream of set up drops – that is, high enough for the

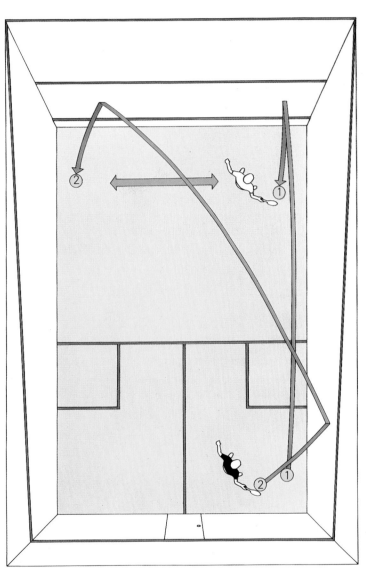

Diagram 3: Straight drop and angle combined with straight hit and cross court hit (see page 32 for text). The back court player hits a straight drop (1) then an angle (2). The front court player hits straight from the drop (1) and cross court from the angle (2).

SHOT ROUTINES

STRAIGHT LOB/DROP AND ANGLE

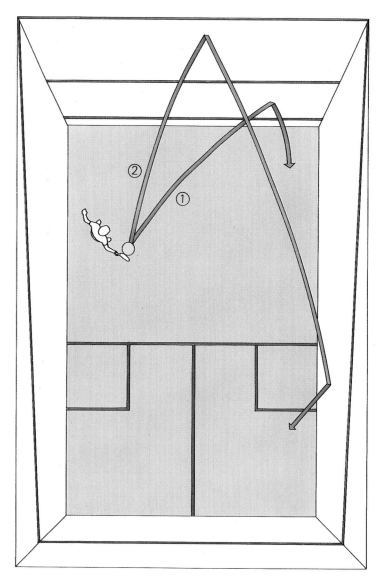

Diagram 4: **Two angles. The player in the front court feeds a short ball (1) to his partner at the back, followed by a deeper ball (2). See Diagram 5 for the back court player's shots.**

player to get to the ball. The player should move in and out to the ball, two paces being about the right amount of movement.

Make sure that you do not become static when doing this exercise as this renders it almost worthless!·

Straight lob and volley drop

This a very difficult practice needing advanced control and technique – and a lot of concentration!

It is more usual to think of the lob as a cross court shot, but a straight lob is a very useful alternative since, if played accurately, it has the advantage of being close to the side wall. This shot should be played high, close to the wall and without pace.

The back court player plays the volley drop off the lob, a difficult proposition if the lob is well played.

The straight lob is not often used in matches, but it is worth practising since it has the advantages of making time and of making your opponent play off no pace and off a ball close to the wall.

The volley drop needs excellent timing and control but it is a shot that, once mastered, can be easily used, especially as a return of serve. It will always be a high risk shot – but don't let that discourage you.

Straight drop and angle – straight hit and cross court hit

This practice calls for advanced skills. The back court player may act as a coach/feeder or, if both players are evenly matched and of a similar high standard, may play the shots as well as possible.

The back court player hits a straight drop, followed by an angle. The straight drop must be played with touch, otherwise it will force the front court player into the wrong position. The front court player will hit straight and low from the straight drop and cross court and low from the angle, back in the direction of his or her partner. (See diagram 3 on page 31.)

The front court player must concentrate on the accuracy of the two shots and the back court player must do the same if playing the shots and not feeding.

STRAIGHT DROP/ANGLES/VOLLEYING

If the balls are being fed from the back, the coach/feeder may play the drop and angle in any order. This will have the effect of making the player at the front work much harder and of stressing the need for him or her to watch carefully behind.

Another useful variation to this practice is that the coach may set up a ball for the straight volley instead of the drop shot feed.

Straight drop plus angle with straight hit plus cross court lob

This practice follows on easily from the previous one. The differences are that the cross court hit becomes a lob and both players have to move.

The front player has the choice of hitting straight or lobbing cross court, off which shots the back player will play a straight drop or an angle. Both players will need to watch carefully what the other is doing. This practice also is for players with advanced skills.

Two angles

This practice needs a feeder who sets up a short ball followed by a deeper ball off which the player plays an angle at the front of the court followed by one deeper in the court (see diagrams 4 and 5).

Sympathetic and controlled feeding will encourage easy rhythmical movement, although the positioning is not easy, particularly at the front. This practice encourages the player to use the short angle.

Co-operative cross court volleying

An excellent practice to improve control of the racket head and sharpness in the use of the racket is to have two players volleying co-operatively to each other cross court from a position on the mid court line (see diagram 6 on page 34). The ball should be hit with medium strength on or about the cut line.

Advanced players can carry out this practice at pace, but players of lesser ability can take it at a much slower speed and still gain a lot from it.

This type of practice also has the advantage of quickly highlighting any deficiencies in racket head control.

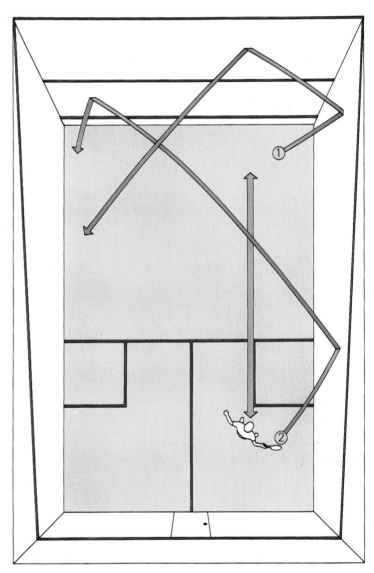

Diagram 5: Two angles (cont'd). The back court player moves to the front to play an angle (1) off the short ball fed by the partner (see Diagram 4), and moves back to play the second, deeper angle.

SHOT ROUTINES

Diagram 6: Two routines for co-operative volleying. From the front of the court, where the routine can be made more difficult by increasing the pace of the shots. From deeper in court, which is more difficult because of the height of the ball.

You will not always be able to get into the best position to hit into the cross court nick. The crucial point to remember is that you should be still as you play the shot. You will also find it advantageous to open up the shoulders to allow the ball to be hit in the correct direction.

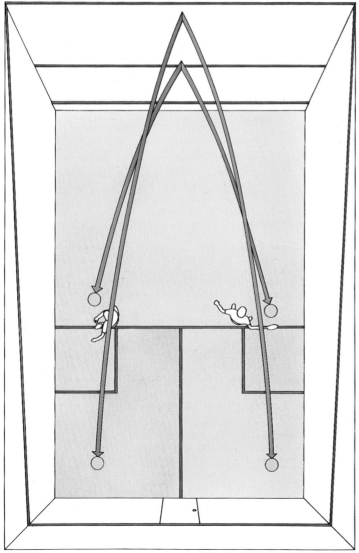

Co-operative volleying from deeper in the court

This practice is similar in concept to the preceding one, but with a different aim. The volleys will be higher and deeper and without the same pace, and will be played from just behind the back of the box (see illustration). Nonetheless, the difficulty in the practice is the timing. The ball will often be played from high, testing positions, the sort familiar when receiving service.

Advanced level players will be aiming at width, besides maintaining rhythm and relaxation through the swing.

Cross court nicks

As you develop as a player the need to finish rallies becomes more and more important, as your chances to finish occur with less and less frequency at higher levels of play.

Hitting the ball into the nick – the join between the floor and the wall – so that the ball rolls along the floor is the best way of winning a rally. Needless to say, it is a very demanding

CROSS COURT NICKS/DOUBLE FEEDS

skill and even though some players have a natural flair for hitting the nick, they still need practice.

The player can take up positions forward in the court – no further forward than the mid court line and any position deeper than that.

The feeder sets up a range of volleys, varying in pace, height and placement, which the player attempts to hit into the cross court nick (see illustration). The feeder will have to be alert and skilful to maintain the practice and if the player is accurate in his shots then the task may be bordering on the impossible. Hitting nicks is best done regularly but in short doses – perhaps at the end of a practice session.

Double feeds

These practices require two feeders and one player. They are physically demanding if properly executed, so you and your partners can take it in turns to play and feed.

The player's aim throughout the following five suggested practices is to concentrate on correct technique and proper footwork. All the practices are best performed with a left foot lead on the forehand and a right foot lead on the backhand – for a right-hander, that is.

1. For the first routine, the feeders position themselves behind the service box and their job is to set up a ball on to the front wall which will present the player with the opportunity to hit the ball straight and low and close to the side wall (see diagram 7).

The feed should be light, so that it does not come back too far in the court, and should be

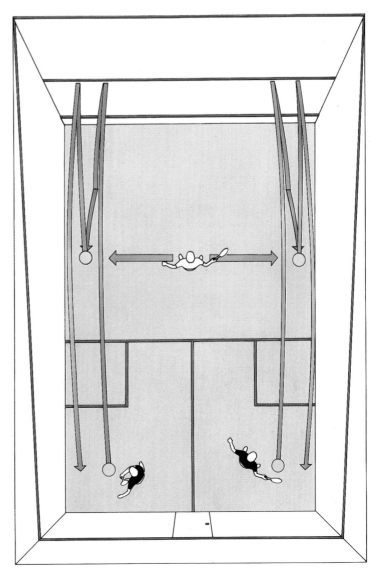

Diagram 7: Double feed, practice 1. The two feeders stand behind the service box and in turn set up a ball on the front wall for the player to hit off the bounce, straight and low and close to the side wall.

DOUBLE FEEDS

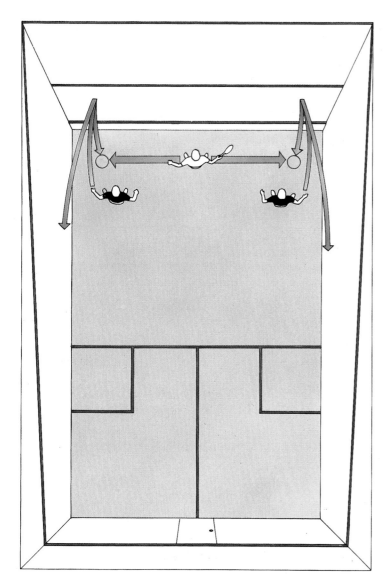

Diagram 8: **Double feed, practice 3. The player makes drop shots alternately on the forehand and backhand side from balls fed by his two partners.**

quite wide. Any ball not wide enough will be too close to the player's body and will therefore force him or her into playing from the wrong position.

The two feeders must time their feeds for the benefit of the player to enable him to play the ball properly. The ball should be there when the player arrives. The feeder positioned on the backhand side may find it helpful to make the feed with a forehand stroke.

2. The second routine involves the feeders and the player adopting the same positions. The feeders now have to set up a light, wide volley for the player to hit to the same targets as in the first practice. The volley practice will show up any deficiencies in the player's racket head control and inexperienced players may find it quite difficult (just as the feeders may have problems supplying consistently accurate feeds to the player).

3. The feeders move forward to the front of the court, as does the player. The feeders now hand feed the ball on to the front wall, inviting the player to move from side to side playing two drop shots into the corners (see diagram 8).

4. The fourth routine also involves two drop shots, this time played off balls fed on to the cut line by hand so that the player can volley the drop shots. The drop shots do not present a difficulty for the feeders in either this practice or in No. 3, though the feeders must concentrate well enough to ensure that they get the timing right.

5. The final practice brings the two feeders back to their original positions in the court.

MATURING SKILLS

"What has helped me maintain my playing standards over the past few years is regular practice, to make sure the racket skills remain intact. Although I have lost a little speed, I have found that my ability to use the ball has improved, providing the necessary compensation." – *Alex Cowie, former international and British over-35 Open champion; England Women's team manager*

This time they play a short and quite demanding feed towards the front corners. Obviously the timing and placement are of crucial importance. Off these two feeds the player has the choice of either hitting straight and low, as previously practised, a drop shot, or a high, straight, floated ball. Provided the feeders are sufficiently skilful and alert, they should experience few problems.

Going solo

You may sometimes lack a partner, so it is useful to have practices which can profitably be done solo.

1. Hitting the ball into the service box is a well known discipline, the main advantage of which is that it provides a target area large enough for players of modest standard.

   Since the service box is behind the mid court line it does give you time to adjust your feet and prepare your swing correctly, both of which are essential aspects of the practice; it also has the advantage that you can count the number of valid shots, thus assessing your progress. Better players who find the practice too simple can increase the pace of their hitting or reduce the target area.

2. Volleying to yourself is a good exercise in control which can be carried out at any distance from the front wall. It is an excellent test of control to begin volleying close to the front wall and work back towards the mid court line without stopping. Volleying from much deeper than the mid court line becomes increasingly difficult. However, the practice does not have to be carried out with movement and can be done at set places in the court to provide you with different problems.

   The pace of the volleys can be increased to suit your ability. This practice also aids concentration and watching the ball.

3. Take up a central mid court position a pace or so in front of the 'T', and then volley from side to side (see diagram 9). This calls for quick manoeuvring and strict control of your racket face. If you are counting the sequence, then any two volleys on the same side end the sequence. You are allowed to move, but if you are controlling the ball properly movement should be minimal.

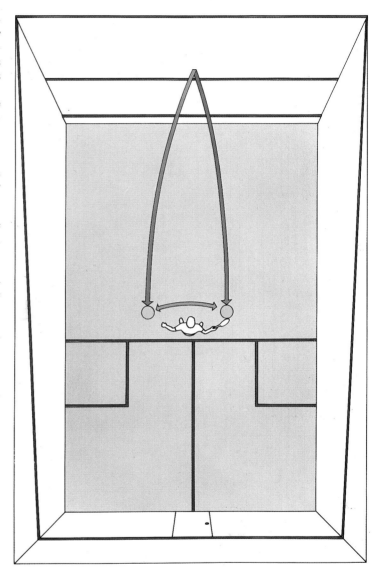

Diagram 9: Going solo, practice 3. The player volleys from side to side, with minimum movement.

PRACTICE GAMES

DOWN THE WALLS/ONE V TWO/THREE BALL

Having practised your shots individually, you should now combine them and try them out in practice games. None of the following games is specific insomuch as each one incorporates several of the shots covered in Chapter 1. You should use these games as part of your practice programme. Used properly they will show you how to put shots together and help you build an effective game.

This chapter is broken down into three parts. The first section provides a selection of games for players of similar ability. This is followed by a section on what are called 'condition games', which place certain constraints on the participants and can be great fun for players of mixed ability. Finally, there's a brief look at how doubles can be used profitably as a means of practice.

Playing down the walls

If the service box outer line is extended to the front and back of the court, it forms a rectangle which runs the entire length of the wall. You can then play a game within the confines of this area and practise all manner of straight shots.

The game involves keeping the ball close to the wall with a variety of drop shots, hard hits and floated lobbed balls – all of which should have been well practised!

To begin the game, the server should stand in front of the mid court line and serve the ball deep. The game is then on and continues until an error or a winning shot occurs. You may adopt scoring systems to suit. Another advantage of this game is that it can occupy four people on a court.

There are variations on the game; one is that both players have to play the ball above the cut line. This variation involves a great deal of volleying, control and, when the rallies are as sustained as they should be to make the game worthwhile, patience.

Another variation is playing every ball, except the service, below the cut line. This is a game calling for sharpness of stroke and of movement. Drops and low hitting of the ball, both desirable, are an essential feature of this game.

It makes a neat package to put these three

games together, the last two variations first, finishing with the game without restriction, bringing into play the requirements of the first two.

One versus two

In many practices players are not under much stress, so it is useful to be able to create situations where players do have to play shots under physical pressure.

An effective practice is to have one player against two opponents. It needs little imagination to realize that the single player will generally have to work very hard!

This is also a chance to bring together players of different standards since the single player can be of a much higher standard than the pair. If the three players are of similar standard, then they can play the part of the single player in turn.

From a competitive point of view the single player often does better than you might expect, since the pair can easily be lulled into a false sense of relative inactivity and fail to move forward.

Three ball

This practice game involves three players playing one after the other. It has the advantages of allowing a little more time to play shots, of encouraging fluent movement and creating long rallies.

The scoring system is the reverse of the usual one, since players score a point for making an error or failing to retrieve the ball, the player ending with the lowest score being the winner.

The loser of each rally serves and anyone playing out of turn or failing to play the ball at the right time also scores. There is to be no setting up of the ball to the disadvantage of any player!

Lisa Opie moves in to attack on her favourite side.

One for the volley

This is a practice game which needs a reliable person to keep the score, since scoring is crucial to its success.

Essentially the game is played normally, but to encourage players to volley one point is scored for every successful volley as well as one point for winning a rally. The scorer therefore has to keep alert all the time. Because players are trying to volley the game tends to be played at a pressured pace, thus helping to improve the players' movement and sharpness around the court.

Front court game

This game is played in front of the mid court line, the purpose being to sharpen up the reflexes and racket control.

The front half of the court is divided and each player must play the ball back to the other side, using any combination of shot and hitting the ball as hard as they wish. The ball

may not pass an opposing player on the wrong side of the line or above shoulder height.

No advantage is to be gained from the 'service' and the scoring system may be adapted as required.

CONDITION GAMES

Condition games, in which one or both players play within certain limits, are a very good source of practice. An added asset is that it is possible to combine players of varying standards, adjusting the conditions accordingly.

Straight v normal

'Normal' refers to the player who is allowed to play without restriction. The other player has to play down the side on which he addresses the ball. This player's purpose will be to get the ball close to the wall and to vary the shots from short to long, from power to touch. Tightness and variety win the points.

CONDITION GAMES

The player without restriction will be in position early, ready to take advantage of any looseness of play. Although this game appears heavily biased in favour of the unrestricted player, if the straight player plays well it may not be so one-sided.

Below the cut line

In this game, one player can play without restriction against the other hitting the ball below the cut line. Alternatively, both may play under this condition.

The emphasis is therefore on short, sharp rallies with low hitting and drop shots being central to the game. Because the ball is never high in the air, there is sustained pressure on the player hitting below the cut line who will have little time between shots.

This game is particularly useful for practising the discipline of keeping the ball low over the tin.

Above the cut line

The emphasis here is understandably completely different from that of the previous game. There will be high balls played with less power, which will invite volleying. Both players will have time in which to play their shots and if the game is well played there will be long rallies.

It is important to maintain accuracy: wide, high balls cross court and tight straight balls are what you should aim for, since this will be the way rallies are won.

The game is not too difficult to play but difficult enough to play well, so it is an appropriate one for varying standards of play-

er. It is designed to encourage easy, fluent stroking of the ball. If only one player is under the restriction he or she will be under considerable pressure since winning the rallies will be difficult.

Behind the mid court line

Although this bears certain similarities to the previous game, it is appreciably more difficult and a more defensive practice. Once the ball finds its way into the back corners – and since it can be hit harder that will happen more easily – it will be much more of a problem to return it deep again. For advanced players, however, it will not be too difficult, since straightening the ball out will be a skill they have developed.

If only one player is under restriction he or she can be put under considerable pressure, so it is a good practice for players of different standard.

Angles and cross courts

I have found this a particularly successful exercise since, well played, it seems to appeal to players' imaginations at the same time as providing for plenty of movement, twisting and turning.

One player (or more usually both) is restricted to playing any variety of angles and cross court balls. They often produce angles they would not normally have considered, from unlikely positions, which is a stimulus.

Angles only

This is not to be taken too seriously since it produces unlikely situations, but it can be a bit of fun and quite relaxing, especially if both players are playing angles.

It is probably more valid if one player only plays under restriction. The disparity between the two players in this instance may be very marked.

Returning the serve straight

The player receiving serve has to return the service straight – any variety of straight ball. The return of serve must land in the rectangle down the side wall as defined by the extension of the service box line to the front and back of the court. Once the ball lands in that area, the rally is played out down the wall inside the rectangle. If the receiver fails to place the ball in the designated area, he loses the rally.

As a variation the receiver may be permitted to return the serve inside either rectangle – the rally still to be played down the wall.

Any practice that calls for an accurate return of service is extremely useful.

Playing the ball into either rectangle

In this instance the game is normal with the condition that the ball has to land at all times in either of the two rectangles defined by the extension of the service box.

This will help to stress the importance of not playing shots down the middle of the court. Although the two wide rectangles provide a generous area, the practice is still sufficiently difficult to be testing even for players of advanced standard.

Lob and drop

This is probably most successful with only one player under condition.

Although being confined to the lob and drop sounds a difficult proposition, advanced players allowed to play the shots from anywhere on the court are able to handle the game well, and may even be able to give the player not under restriction a considerable run round.

Needless to say, this is valuable practice of these two skilful shots.

Continuous squash

This practice makes heavy physical demands, where the quality of the squash may be difficult to sustain.

Basically the idea is that the game, once underway, does not stop. Each player should attempt to play the ball normally, but if they are unable to reach it before the second bounce that is of no account and they should play it as it occurs.

If the rally breaks down, then the nearest player has the responsibility of putting it back into play immediately, obviously in a co-operative manner. Amidst the continuous

action, both players should attempt to maintain as high a quality of squash as they can.

DOUBLES

Doubles is a splendid game in its own right, as well as very useful as a practice, and as the game grows in popularity so the number of tournaments, both open and club, increases. The creation of a British Championship for women and men gave the game a boost and it has gone from strength to strength.

The involvement of four players instead of the customary two has clear advantages, both in tournament and practice, and whereas there might be too great a disparity between two single players, the physical confines of the doubles game can bring them together. This could mean in a practice game, for instance, that younger players of ability could well play with high quality older players with obvious benefits.

As a game doubles requires advanced technique because of the confined space and it is not a game for unskilled players with dubious swings. Apart from the fact that the game can be dangerous if the players are clumsy, technique is what will in the end win doubles matches.

But it is not only a test of technique – it is also of movement, since failure to clear the ball will ruin any game of doubles. So in using doubles as a practice, you will be gaining experience in both of these crucial areas.

If you are at the end of training sessions doubles will relieve some of the physical pressure without any lessening of the need for ball control and skill. It does require high concentration, so even if you are physically less than fresh, you will still need to apply yourself mentally. It is not a good idea for all practice to be too heavy and serious, so doubles with its potential for lighter moments may also provide some useful light relief.

The game, at its best, requires precision, patience, concentration and judgment to know when and how to attack. The best combination of doubles players generally involves one steady and persistent player with one who has the ability to finish or at least attack at the appropriate moments.

GETTING IN SHAPE
WEIGHT TRAINING/RUNNING

The physical demands that the game of squash will make on you are such that you will have to pay some attention to fitness. Squash requires such a combination of speed, stamina and agility that most people will be found wanting in some aspect or other. You must take stock of your deficiences so that you can gear your physical training accordingly. There is always a tendency in training, as in practising, to work on strengths: players will invariably have the capacity to delude themselves and they may have genuine difficulties recognizing their strengths and weaknesses. Not everyone has the ability to be objective.

Not many sports make the excessive demands on players that squash does and one aspect of the game responsible for this is that resting periods are few and far between. Squash players hit every other ball; the rest between games hardly gives the player time to towel down and the speed at which the game is played allows no respite. Compare that with the anonymous role of the footballer who disappears for large parts of the game or the tennis player who spends more time serving and towelling down than in actual play.

World class squash players are athletically first rate. The rigorous training schedules of Jonah Barrington, the natural athleticism of Geoff Hunt and the economical movement of Jahangir Khan, the last three World No. 1's, are testimony enough to this. Although these three represent the very top of the game, the demands on players of international, national, county and even good club standards to be in shape are real enough and exist to a greater or lesser degree.

It will be of little value to have extreme racket skill without the physical conditioning to support it. Equally, to make a god of training is not good for you either.

The danger of being over-trained and over-muscled is that the risk of breaking down and becoming unsound will be increased. If the right balance of training is achieved, it is likely to extend your playing life – always allowing for your having retained enthusiasm!

The average player good enough to play matches in club teams, with other demands

on his time, may have less opportunity to fit in any physical work to enhance his playing prospects. However, many squash clubs have weight rooms or a small gymnasium, which makes that a lot easier. Training can be tacked on after a game. Sometimes lunchtime provides the right opportunity, and has the additional benefit of restricting possibilities of over-indulging! Below are outlined a few training ideas to help you improve your physical fitness.

Weight training
Much profitable work can be done within the confines of a weight room: the combination of lifting lighter weights and doing physical exercises is an ideal one for squash players: simple lifts together with squat thrusts, star jumps, burpees and trunk curls cannot fail to develop strength and pace. Anyone new to such exertions should build up gradually, increasing repetition of weights and numbers of exercises as fitness levels improve. This form of training need not and should not occupy too much of your time: twenty minutes in earnest will be sufficient. Strength, speed and the explosive movement required for squash will all be improved as a result.

Running
Running does not require too much time or special facility, though the surface on which you run is very important. Hard surfaces, such as roads, are not desirable since they may cause shin and knee problems. I have always found grass as good a surface as any. A football, or preferably a rugby, pitch lends itself to running suitable for squash. Using the 22m (24yd) and the halfway line you can do repeti-

tion running interspersed with rests such as walking to the next mark, which are better for you than standing and resting.

Running long distances, apart from being time-consuming, will have the effect of slowing you down. Stamina may be increased, but pace will be lost in the process. Try short runs of up to 1.5-2.5km (1-1½ miles) with emphasis on a strong finish, or interval running, consisting of repeated short runs of, say, 25, 50, 100m (27, 54, 109yd). These can be carried out with brief rests; for example, run 25m (27yd) walk 25m (27yd) and so on. Short distance running should be done hard. In that way you do not have to spend a lot of time on this form of training.

Movement on court

The court itself provides an immediate facility for training, and has the advantage of allowing you to gear the training to simulating movements to those in an actual game.

Working from the centre, movements can be made into various areas of the court, usually the corners, with recovery to the middle after each movement. It is helpful to have someone call out the required movements and also to encourage you to maintain pace as the pressure mounts. A simple means of organizing this type of training is to number the relevant areas and have your partner call out the number. You may simulate a stroke or, if you wish, just move, though the racket may help you produce a more realistic position. (See diagram 10.)

The court may also be used for running from front to back, on the way touching the lines, existing or imaginary. The bending required increases physical exertion and is squash related. Other worthwhile forms of exercise are those already mentioned in combination with weight training and skipping.

Stretching

There are a number of stretching exercises that can be executed quite easily and are designed to improve mobility and flexibility around the court. Below are a few suggestions, but first some general points. When you do these or other stretching exercises, your

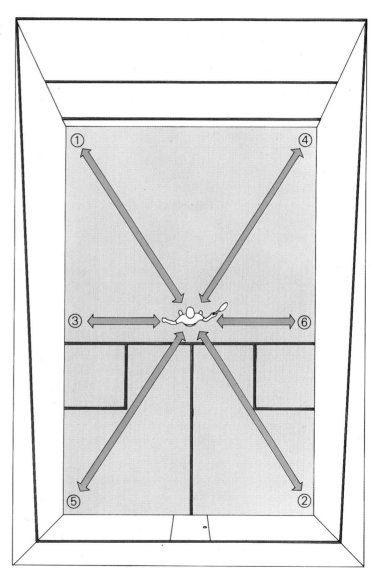

Diagram 10: You can improve your mobility and speed around the court through movement training. Designate areas of the court, as shown, position yourself in the centre and get your partner to call out the numbers at random. You may simulate a stroke or just move to the area. Return to the centre after each movement.

GETTING IN SHAPE

STRETCHING

movements should be smooth, not quick or jerky. Hold each stretch for a count of five, relax and then repeat. Stretch both sides of your body. Always breathe comfortably and try to relax. If you strain or hold your breath you'll most likely do yourself more harm than good. Be particularly careful if you are stretching to aid recovery from an injury: stretch almost to the point of pain, but no more!

Passive:

1. In a crouching position, bend forwards and place your fingers under your toes. Raise your bottom slowly and push back with your knees, keeping hold of your toes. Hold. Slowly break the position.

2. Standing with your feet together, arm's length from a wall, place both hands, palms flat, against the wall. Keeping your arms straight and pushing against the wall, bend one leg forward at the knee, raising your heel. Now bend the other leg, shifting your weight on to the ball of your foot, heel raised. Hold this position with both legs bent. Repeat, but this time starting with the other leg.

3. Stretch one leg behind you. Keeping it straight, lower your hips as far as you can, bending your other leg. Hold. Repeat exercise with other leg. (A variation is to hold your arms out behind you once you are in the lowered position.)

4. Stand with your feet apart. Bend your left knee, keeping your right leg straight. Hold. Release and repeat for other side.

5. Raise both arms above your head and join hands. From the waist, bend your body first to one side then to the other, going as far as you can without straining. Hold. Straighten up and begin exercise again, starting with the other side.

6. Sit down on your heels. Place your hands behind you on the floor. Raise your bottom, keeping your head back, and pushing down with your hands. Hold and then release.

7. Try the splits – but carefully – using your hands for support. Go down as far as you can, but don't force it. You'll get there with patience and practice.

8. Lie on your front and place both hands

beneath your shoulders, palms down. Slowly raise your trunk by pushing up until your arms are straight. Your hips and lower body should remain on the floor – this isn't a press up.

9. Sit on the floor with your back straight. Keep your right leg straight out in front of you and bring your left leg up until you can place your left foot against the upper inside of your right thigh. Slowly raise your arms above your head, lean forwards and take hold of your right leg, without strain. Bend both elbows outwards, pull your trunk slowly downwards as far as you are able, again without strain. Hold. Release leg and slowly straighten up. Repeat for the other side.

10. Sit down. Stretch both legs out in front of you. Take hold of your toes (or as near as you can get without bending your legs), bend your elbows and hold.

11. Stand on the edge of a step. Raise yourself on the ball of your left foot while pushing down with the heel of your right foot. Repeat with the other leg.

12. Get down on all fours. Stretch one leg out straight behind you as far as you can and hold. Repeat with the other leg.

13. Adopt a shoulder stand position. Lower your legs as slowly as possible, keeping them straight.

14. Lying flat on your back, take hold of your ankles with your hands and raise your bottom, arching your back as much as possible. Hold. Slowly break position.

For mobility

1. Stand with your feet slightly apart and twist from side to side from the waist.

2. Arm circling: forwards and backwards with alternate arms and then with both arms together.

Jahangir Khan in an unusual situation – at full stretch!

3. Leg swings: support yourself against a wall or rail and swing first one leg then the other forwards and backwards to loosen up your hip joints.

4. Neck rolls: drop your shoulders – do not hunch them – and roll your head sideways around your shoulders slowly, first in one direction then in the other. As far as you can but without straining, nod your head forwards and back, and from side to side.

The point to make about any of these suggestions is that they need not take up much time; they do not necessarily require any special facility and can be fitted round a game of squash quite easily. Nor are they outside any player's capacities, since the pace and intensity can be increased or lessened according to the player's needs and fitness. As with so many things in life, 'a little and often' is good advice, with regularity added for good measure. One thing is sure, improvement in your physical condition is almost guaranteed to bring about improvement in your playing standard.

Now that we've discussed long-term preparation in the form of training, we'll look at the short term build-up to a match.

MATCH PREPARATION
PRELIMINARIES

Players are all different in the amount of work and match play they can undertake, so one of your first requirements is to understand your own needs. Some players will be able to absorb heavy match play and may even thrive on it, while others will be undermined by it. There is little point in playing match after match when below form, since a string of losses will make you lose confidence. Nobody thrives on losing, despite the old fashioned public school notion 'it does one good to lose'. Losses happen to all, no matter how good, so no-one needs to go looking for losses on the grounds that they will be a better person for it! Winners, in my experience, are bred on winning.

In preparing for any match, where factors are controllable, exercise control; where they are outside control, do the best you can.

If you are representing your club in county or local leagues you will have plenty to contend with to arrive well prepared for mid-week matches. It's quite likely that your daily work and your domestic situation are not conducive to playing well. A fraught day at the office, much travelling on the day of the game, a row with your nearest and dearest – who would rather you spend the time altogether differently – will not assist your cause. You may not be in a position to do too much about either, though there are those who are influenced in their choice of both by their love of the game. Tommy Steele, for one, doesn't like to work too far from a squash court, so he can take his daily exercise. But it definitely helps to have a hassle-free domestic life to make things easier when you are required for matches – unless you are one of those rare birds who can turn the feelings involved in these situations to advantage.

If your work is generally hectic, then the best thing you can develop is the ability to switch off once you are on your way to the match. Easier said than done, I hear you say, but worth working at, since it should improve your chances of a win and it may even increase life expectancy! If the match is very important, then a day off work would be the answer – unless you spend the day worrying about what you should be doing at work!

Final practice
It will never come amiss, should it prove practical, to hit a ball on the day of the game. Half an hour at lunchtime may be a possibility, but if that is difficult it may be easier to get to the venue a little early and do it then. The hitting of the ball, often alone, will help you get your eye in, groove your swing, hit whatever shots take your fancy and loosen you up physically. If this isn't possible, you should have either played or practised on the day before the match. It is not a good idea to go into a match without having hit the ball for two or three days – that would be a preparation, or lack of it, designed only to assist your opponent.

Eating
Eating before squash matches is a personal matter: some can eat substantially, though obviously not too close to a match, while others prefer to eat much less. It is probably equally undesirable to eat too much or nothing at all. The sensible course is to be aware of what suits you best and stick to that.

Equipment
It should hardly need saying, but your equipment, racket, especially the grip, shoes and any other significant item should all be in good working order – though, of course, there may be occasions when faulty equipment might provide a welcome rest! Make sure you cover all eventualities; have spare shirts and rackets, change of footwear, towels and so on all prepared. None of this takes too much time and effort and can easily be done.

Timing your arrival
The time of arrival at the match is another matter worth consideration though, again, you may not always have much choice. Better

PRELIMINARIES

not to arrive at a time when you are liable to be rushed straight on court. It is a good idea to arrive with time to spare but too much may, in some instances, fray your nerves. Some players like to go on first in a match, others prefer to play later. These are matters not easy to control, however, since when you go on court is normally decided by the position you hold in the team. Usually matches are played from the bottom upwards, though there are set orders for county and international matches that vary slightly on that principle.

Team responsibilities

A factor that can certainly affect performance is being called on to mark or referee a match before playing. This may be no serious problem if the match officiated is not well contested, but playing after a long drawn-out, contentious five-setter is not ideal. For sure it would be wise not to mark more than one match before playing, which can occur if you are last on court.

Most squash players' match play will be a combination of individual and team play and while some players are better at playing for themselves, others are better playing for teams. There is no shortage of opportunity to play team squash. Every club has league teams; there are county sides at every age level and international teams for those of the required standard; there are also numerous national team competitions. Many of the players in these teams will play much more team squash than individual tournaments.

If you are a team player you will thrive on the atmosphere of feeling involved with four other players, all of you dependent on each other to achieve the desired result. When the situation requires, you will find the extra and be prepared to extend yourself physically and mentally.

Keeping fresh

Sometimes if a player is playing a tournament he may have to play more than one match a day, so it is important to recharge the batteries, especially if the first win has been hard earned. Freshening up by swilling your face in cold water before going on court again is a beneficial practice. It is also dangerous to stay in the squash club for prolonged periods in such circumstances and a breath of fresh air at appropriate times is a good idea.

Warming up

As the match nears it is necessary to warm up, particularly if you are cold or stiff. Warming up before going on court is, besides assisting a quick start, an insurance against injuries, which are more likely to occur if the muscles are cold and tight. How to warm up is a matter of personal preference. Some may prefer to run if there is suitable space; others may stretch – perhaps a combination of the two is ideal, as running may help the playing of the game and stretching will do that and make movement easier.

Knocking up

The knock up is a continuation of the warm-up process, but now involves the racket, and is a significant part of the preparation for a match. Besides allowing you to hit the ball and get your eye in, it provides an opportunity for you to size up the opposition, though the latter should not be your main preoccupation. It is easy enough to deceive yourself by underestimating an opponent who is a poor technician only to find, to your cost, that he or she is far from easy meat. But to an experienced eye, the knock up will provide a guide to an opponent's real merit. If you are well practised in the art of knocking up you may even be skilful and cunning enough to hide your strengths and veil over your weaknesses, enabling you to strike fear and uncer-

> **BOXING CLEVER**
>
> "I love squash as the last of the great combat sports – head-to-head, boxing without brain damage. The physical requirements are similar to those for boxing, the environment too, and the psychology. The opponent is manoeuvred into a disadvantageous positon, then punished." – *Colin McQuillan, leading squash writer and sports journalist*

tainty into your unsuspecting opponent as the match progresses.

Every player will recognize the personal significance of the knock up: some will feel happier if they are hitting the ball exceptionally well in that five minutes, to others that will not be so important. Whatever the case, the knock up is the time in which you have to become mentally and physically aware of what is required for you to play well and hopefully, win.

Knowledge that your preparation has been thorough will increase your confidence. No-

Bryan Beeson on his way to victory over Ashley Naylor in the 1987 Telesquash final.

thing will feed your uncertainty more than knowing that the necessary work has not been done.

All the racket skill in the world will be worthless if you are not fit enough; likewise, it would be foolish to imagine that being superbly fit without the necessary racket skill is of any use. When you achieve the right combination success will not be far away.

Remember, though, that heading these two major requirements is your mental attitude. If your head cannot stand the pressure, then neither fitness nor racket ability will be much use.

COURT CRAFT

TAKING STOCK

Tactics and awareness go together. If you lack awareness of space, of your opponent's position on the court, of your own abilities and of your opponent's strengths and weaknesses then these are serious deficiencies which you will have to remedy if improvement's your aim. Some players – the lucky ones – have an innate tactical sense, while others are less fortunate in varying degrees. Players who completely lack awareness will need the help of a coach to make tactical observations for them and to school them into acquiring it. The best players seem to have a natural sense of awareness, but there's no reason why it shouldn't be learnt with almost equally good results.

Awareness requires powers of observation as well as self-knowledge and is heightened by observing others. You can help develop your sense of awareness by identifying your strengths and using them wisely, and protecting your weaknesses, at the same time watching for tell-tale signs from your opponent. Experience will point out when you are reading the signs incorrectly or misusing your game. So, basic awareness is the foundation for all tactical appreciation in squash and is behind any tactical move you make on court.

Unlike some sports, there aren't a number of set moves that you can learn and build in to your game – so much depends on factors that change from one game to the next. However, there are several general tactical considerations that you should bear in mind when playing, plus a few tips to put you ahead of the game.

Play in progress

Always take stock of your opponent. You may know something of him or her beforehand; you may have played previously; if not, then the knock-up may give you some clues. Once the game has started you should always try to be aware of how your opponent's game is taking shape. It can be dangerous, however, to be too taken up with your opponent's weaknesses – you should mainly concentrate on using your own strengths. Don't forget that if you rely too much on one area of weakness in your opponent, it may have the unde-

sirable effect of eliminating that weakness and playing him in!

Court conditions

Playing conditions, like opponents, have to be taken into account, since both will affect what tactics need to be employed, and the opponent's ability will determine the amount of control over tactics any player may exercise. If a player is under pressure then there may not be much he can do tactically – especially of a legitimate nature!

Slow, cold conditions favour shots such as the lob and drop both of which are liable to 'die', leaving the opponent with few options but survival. So, faced with cold conditions, it will be useful to have those shots available. The drop is particularly effective against players who are slow to get forward – and there are plenty of those around! So if you are playing a slow-moving opponent in cold conditions and are an expert at the drop, you are in business.

Warmer or hot playing conditions demand more patience, as the rallies are generally more protracted and harder to win. Tactically the danger is to play more negatively. Drop shots will not win such rallies outright, but they must still be played to work your opponent to the front of the court. To win a long rally you must have variety of shot and be able to change pace, either to play a winning shot yourself or to force an error from your opponent.

Even in these days of faster courts they are sufficiently various for playing conditions to be an important tactical consideration. So, early on, take stock of the type of court you are playing on and make the necessary adjustments to your game.

Opening moves

Since the serve and return of serve are the opening shots of any rally, they are highly significant tactically. Although the first requirement is for a reliable, consistent serve, it is the variety, in both pace and direction, which may give you a tactical advantage. Some players, for example, are slow to get out of the way of a ball hit straight at them, so

Qamar Zaman moves in on the backhand, perfectly set up to make full use of his racket skills and awareness.

COURT CRAFT

SIMPLE AIMS

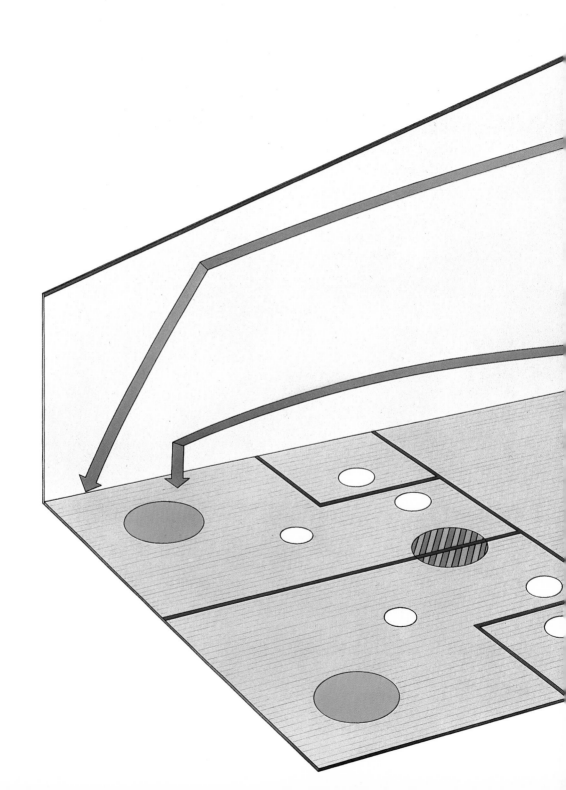

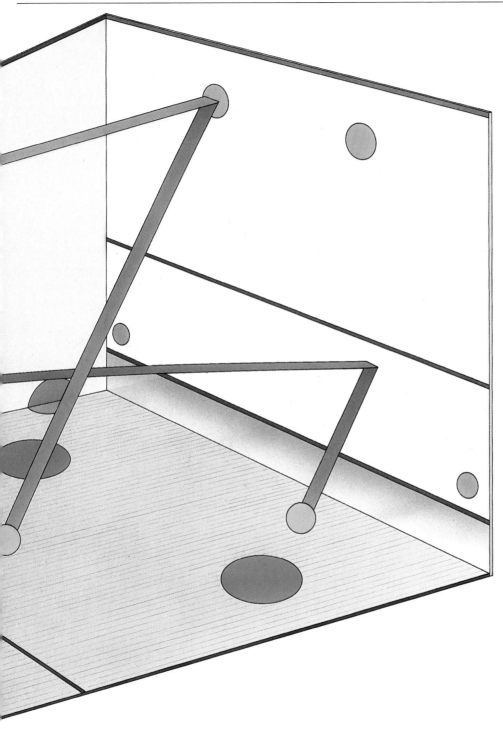

The tactical aims of squash are simple. You play your opponent into disadvantageous positions to pressurize him or her into making an error, and set yourself up to dictate the flow of the game. The best way to achieve these aims is by using the corners of the court. The accompanying illustration shows a few basic ways of doing this, and identifies court positions, the passage of the ball and where to aim.

The positions for serving (white areas across the inner lines of the service box) and receiving (white areas behind the box) leave you well placed near the centre of the court. The large green circles at the front and at the back of the court are basically offensive (dark green) and defensive (light green) positions respectively. After each shot recover to the 'T' position (light and dark green striped area) to cover your opponent's reply.

Balls that go into the corners are played low and close to the side walls; note the target areas (orange) just above the tin on the front wall. The line for an attacking shot into the nick on the forehand side is the orange circle at the front of the side wall where the wall meets the floor.

The serve in squash should not be underestimated and you should try to gain advantage from it. The upper blue line shows the line for the service (forehand; only the point of contact on the front wall for the backhand is shown) that would pose difficulties for your opponent. The ball will drop deep in court and very close to the side wall, making it very awkward to return. Your cross courts (lower blue line) should be played to cause similar problems for your opponent.

COURT CRAFT
THE OPTIONS

that is a serve which may put you on the attack from the outset. It is not unusual, if the serve is cleverly delivered, to hit the receiver with the ball which, besides winning the point for you, has the added psychological advantage of making your opponent look and feel very silly indeed!

Players who can serve high and wide with little pace on to the side wall are sufficiently rare as to cause panic in an opponent and put him or her in all sorts of trouble; see diagram on pages 54-5 for an effective serve path. So, it is worth cultivating a good serve.

Just as the serve may influence the course of any rally so, too, the return, if well-directed, may put the server under pressure from which he might not recover. To have options on the return is crucial, for that will help you deal with a difficult serve and at the same time help you counter-attack.

The quality of attack a receiver may exert depends on the problems the server poses and his own options. Straight returns will stretch the opponent wide, cross courts will cause him to turn and angles will bring him forward, always allowing for them being accurately played.

One of the dangers for players with a tendency to stroke making is to play shots too early. Far better to ease into the match and introduce shots once your timing is assured. It can look spectacular, of course, to begin a match with a series of winners, but they will have to be outright, since your opponent will be at his freshest and capable of picking up most offerings. Tactically, then, it is not policy to go in with guns blazing, even if your confidence is high.

Some players are by disposition quick starters and some slow starters. If you are in the latter category, you should take every neces-sary action to gainsay the dangers of a slow start. There is nothing wrong with being a strong finisher, which slow starters often are! Everyone will know of players who can be almost guaranteed to win if taken the full distance, just as there are players who might as well go home unless they take an early lead.

Shot selection

Knowing when to play shots as a game progresses, selecting the correct shot for any situation, introducing certain shots as your opponent tires are all part of the tactical awareness required by any player, no matter how modest. As the standard of play reaches higher levels, the emphasis changes: whereas lower down the scale a player might get away with loose or badly chosen shots, that no longer holds the higher up you go, until at the very highest levels, opportunities for attack present themselves so rarely that when they do they have to be taken. Such is the precision of play that the opportunity may take no recognizing – it may be a half chance – but the finishing has to be deadly.

To support the tactical appreciation of any one match, or any one rally, you should have the range of shots that will allow you to put that appreciation to good use. It is frustrating to know what to do tactically, but to be without the wherewithal to deliver the goods. Some players' minds are ahead of their physical ability to play the required shot, which is frequently the case with young, developing players.

Changing pace

It is worth remembering that variety in a game may not only be achieved by range of shot, but also change of pace. The latter may be less obvious, but it is no less important for that. Combine the two and you will have sufficient control to take tactical advantage of most situations.

One of the best ways to combat the hard-hitting player, for example, is to take the pace off the ball. Hard hitters do not like to force off balls without pace – but prefer to play off the pace of the ball struck by their opponent. By lobbing and floating the ball around the court

---

LOOSE ENDS

"I like to play the ball in short from all areas of the court and hopefully having put my opponent under some pressure, capitalize on the loose shots I have caused him to make." – *David Pearson*

Lucy Soutter keeps all her options open against world champion Susan Devoy.

– without suggesting that is easy! – hard hitters can easily be frustrated, will snatch at the ball and, if the tactics work, will start putting it in the tin. Once the tactic begins to work there may well be a snowball effect as hard hitters tend not to be able to change course but will continue to thrash away until the bitter end. Unfortunately, a common misconception about squash is that it's all about hitting the ball as hard as possible and rushing around the court like a wild beast. Played properly,

squash is not about brute force, but mental and physical poise, balance, touch, precision and timing.

Flexibility

Every player has a certain style and although this may vary a little depending on the opponent and playing conditions, he will maintain his type of game. One of the things that separates the champions from the also rans is the ability to be flexible. If you can develop tactical

COURT CRAFT

IMPROVISATION

flexibility you will be able to alter your usual game, no matter by how little, to suit any particular occasion. Unfortunately, not many players possess this enviable talent!

Improvisation

The basis of a sound game is technical expertise since under pressure any weaknesses in your technique will be revealed. But built on to the top of this soundness should be the ability to improvise, since not every circumstance you will meet will lend itself to the production of pure technique.

Improvisation calls for the ability to change direction in the course of any one match, according to the playing conditions, the ball and above all the opponent. That will mean changes of pace, variations of shot and changes of tactics.

Things happen fast in squash, and the ball may not always be in a position where you can draw on correct technique. It may, for instance, be struck hard straight at you. Then you will need to improvise to get the racket into

the best position as quickly as possible without out the help of more appropriate footwork. Sometimes, in such a circumstance when there is no time to adjust your feet, the ability to bend your body will help to allow some room for the racket (see illustrations). Do be aware of the value of body movement, since remaining rigid and upright will more likely than not lead to error.

Allied to the ability to manoeuvre the racket will be the ability to move it at speed. The dangers of slow manipulation of the racket are obvious and if you recognize this weakness in your own play you should do all you can to remedy it.

If you lack the ability to improvise mentally and physically you will be hampered by inflexibility and will be at a loss against the more inventive and original of your opponents. If inflexibility is a natural failing it will be difficult to put right; but it may be the product of negative and unimaginative coaching. The coach must ensure that while he is seeking to establish sound technical principles he in no

Right and far right: You may not always have time to move your feet to avoid a ball struck directly at you. It is at such a time that you will appreciate the desirability of being flexible. Whether you're playing on the forehand or backhand side, bend your body to allow space for the racket so you can volley the return.

way curbs the natural tendency of his players to make shots or play with a sense of adventure, nor should he discourage improvised play at appropriate times. Coaches should liberate their charges. The fear of making an error or of losing will inhibit a player and stifle any natural ability he or she may have. I recall the famous Irish rugby player Mike Gibson recounting how the equally famous coach Carwyn James once told him never to be frightened of making mistakes, and how grateful he was for that advice.

While the need to improvise successfully with your racket is of vital importance, you must use this in harmony with a basis of sound technique. It is not enough to play a game full of improvisations. It may work up to a point, because your opponents will not be accustomed to such a game, but it will certainly provide limitation to high standard.

Jamie Hickox, four times British U23 champion and England international, is one of the best examples of a player with the ability to improvise, though at times when he is not in his best form he gets some disastrous results, probably because he cannot fall back on a basic technique which might see him through lack of form.

As a coach, I often hear 'Jahangir doesn't play the shot in the way you are teaching me'. What in fact the professional is doing is improvising under pressure since it is when the pressure is on a player that the need to improvise will be greatest.

Advice from the sidelines

Although the rest of one minute between games (two minutes between fourth and fifth) is a very short period of time, you can nevertheless use it to listen to some good advice. It has to be said, though, that what is said be-

The author tells Alex Cowie just what is required.

tween games to players is not always tactical – often encouragement and motivation are needed more.

It is crucial, though, that those advisers, be they coaches, players, friends or parents, know what they are talking about and that is certainly not always so. They will need to know what they are doing; above all if they offer tactical advice they should have watched the game, hopefully not subjectively, have isolated deficiencies in your performance, recognized any weaknesses in your opponent's game and should be able in the short time allowed to put over important tactical points (not too many) to you, even though you may not always be receptive and may be stressed and fatigued.

If you have no one in your corner – and that will often be so – you will have to make your own evaluations, which may be difficult in the hurly burly of the match. You will have only a minute in which to gather your thoughts, stiffen your resolve and come to tactical decisions.

It goes without saying that you will certainly be better off with help than without it – provided the person offering it knows what he or she is doing!

TROUBLESHOOTING YOUR FAULTS

FOOTWORK

Faults can be divided into two sorts: positioning and racket. The emphasis I have put on correct footwork in the practice routines indicates how great its importance is. Poor footwork is top of the list above all other weaknesses, since the prospects of playing any shot well will be reduced if your feet are not in a helpful position. Coaches and individual players may well have different ideas about what correct footwork consists of, but it is still important for you to have a clear idea of where your feet ought to be.

If your feet are incorrectly placed in relation to the ball, chances are that you will find yourself being too close to it, which is a serious restriction and will either lead you to error or reduce your options.

Balance

Any squash player needs to play from balanced positions, since lack of balance will cause error and poor strokes and will certainly mean that recovery is made much more dif-

ficult. Lack of balance will also take more out of you physically, since you will use extra effort moving from badly balanced positions. Some players (the athletic ones) may be naturally balanced, but if you lack this advantage you can work at your movement and improve it.

Keeping the feet still

One of the commonest and most destructive faults is playing shots with the feet moving. This failing probably causes more mistakes and badly played shots than any other and the sooner you learn to address the ball in a still position the better. Watching players who move well, it is difficult to believe that they are ever still but close inspection will show you that this is so. That wonderful stroke maker Qamar Zaman, whose movement readily shows how still a player should be when addressing the ball, is worth watching for this particular quality, since his movement is sharper and more staccato than some and

Gawain Briars, being very tall, appreciates the need to get down. His opponent here is Ross Thorne.

this tends to highlight the stillness when he plays his shots.

Overrunning the ball

If you do not learn to stay still you will find yourself overrunning the ball, which will lead to your having to play the ball behind your feet, and thus often hooking your wrist, which may be acceptable as improvisation, but is not as established technique. Overrunning the ball is a characteristic failing of players who have a tendency to rush, so mistiming their arrival at the ball.

Running directly at the ball

A tendency to run directly at the ball may well lead you into trouble. If the ball is travelling into the corner and you follow it you will find yourself short of room to swing the racket and be unlikely to be able to produce your intended shot. Leaving room to play, especially when moving into the back of the court, is something you must be aware of.

OFFICIAL VIEW

"Although I'm mainly occupied with the organizational and refereeing side of squash, I do feel that the game is often misunderstood. Because there is a benefit in being error-free, which some players have developed, the very high skill levels of many players go unrecognized. At the top the game is far more attractive and pleasing than it is given credit for, and the professionalism of the players – in the best sense of that word – often goes unrewarded." – *David Stevenson, international referee and administrator*

Blind spots

The advice to watch the ball may seem obvious but apart from watching the ball as you are about to hit it, you must also watch the ball as your opponent prepares to strike. Unlike in many other games, this means looking behind. Developing the ability to watch well and profit from it will lead to you having that magical quality of being able to 'read the game'. Anticipation is just another name for this (see illustration).

Controlling the racket

The faults so far discussed have been of movement. Of equal importance is the avoidance of problems with the racket. Basic faults, caused by turning the wrist, are the closing and opening of the racket face. Closing the face is perhaps the more common error, and leads inevitably to the ball going downwards, very often into the tin. It happens especially on the deeper forehand angle.

Opening the racket face has the obvious effect of hitting the ball upwards. Although it may not cause a direct error, it will leave the ball set up on the front wall for your opponent to punish easily. If the racket face is open too much on such shots as the lob and the serve, it may well be a direct cause of error.

As with other aspects of the game, the subtleties of racket head control will come more easily to some players, but they can be learnt by those with less natural abilities.

Always watch closely what is going on behind you during play. It will help you develop that most difficult skill: anticipation. You should always be ready to move, in any direction, so keep your options open by not having your feet on the same plane.

TROUBLESHOOTING YOUR FAULTS

RACKET CONTROL

Ross Norman winds up a backhand.

A well balanced position showing a controlled follow through with the racket head up. The head and upper body should not come up too soon or too violently after you've hit the ball.

Preparation and follow through

The preparation of the racket and the ensuing follow through are two technical areas where faults are common. It is by no means unusual to see preparation of the racket when the arm is too straight, which produces a wide and dangerous looking swing. The preparation of a straight-armed swing is of no value to you in the production of your shots, but it may intimidate your opponent!

The follow through can cause some players as many difficulties as the preparation. A common error is when the player loses control of the racket after contact with the ball, resulting in a follow through that is, again, either too wide and dangerous or one that may, and frequently does, finish up too high and above the head. Both of these may look impressive to the uninitiated, but neither will be of any assistance to you in achieving the main aim of a correct follow through, which is to get your racket quickly under control again so you are prepared for the next stroke (see illustration right).

Dropping the wrist

Not surprisingly, control of the wrist is what most affects racket head control. Getting the required amount of turn to open and close the racket face, depending on the shot, is one element of wrist control. An equally important factor, and a common failing, is to drop the wrist, especially on the backhand side. As the shots, particularly the drop and the short angle, are being played, the wrist drops and the racket swings towards the floor in a pendulum-like movement. This serious fault is essentially a technical problem and is one that you may learn to cope with simply by being aware of it as a weakness. But, if you play in this way, you will find that it will let you down when the pressure is on – and that is precisely the time when you need your technique to hold up.

Dropping the wrist occurs more on the backhand side, but on the forehand side there is a danger that as preparation of the racket is often lower so the wrist, and therefore the racket head, will be down. This lack of proper

Mark Maclean, rising star of British squash, looks confident under pressure.

preparation will produce its own crop of difficulties.

Composure

Composure is a major requirement of any squash player. Rushing around the squash court in an uncontrolled manner undoubtedly creates its own problems. It follows that if you try to prepare and execute your strokes with similar haste, mistakes will inevitably result. It was, I believe, Doug Saunders, the golfer, who suggested that the best approach to adopt when things are going wrong is to do everything more slowly. He advised golfers to put the tee in the ground slowly, to take time addressing the ball and, finally, to swing slowly. No doubt the last point is the most impor-

tant, but the slow build up is a help. Golf lends itself to going more slowly than does squash, but the same principles apply. In the end the controlled swing is what both the golfer and the squash player are seeking. Certainly the squash player can help himself by taking his time to serve or even by returning unhurriedly to the service box – provided that he does not go so slowly that he is penalized for timewasting! (It seems odd and not a little unfair that the squash player is allowed so little latitude in this respect compared with other games, which are nothing like as strenuous and exacting.) So, ensure that the pace of the game is sensible, and do not allow any tendency you may have to hurry become heightened so that it can be exploited by your opponent.

TROUBLESHOOTING YOUR FAULTS
OVERCUTTING/ADDRESSING THE BALL

One particular area where rushing is evident is in the playing of the volley. The volley produces anxiety in many players. The pressure is on to make the most of what is often an attacking opportunity, and it is often compounded by uncertainty as to whether you have the ability to make the shot at all. Either way, the likelihood is that you will hurry the stroke and snatch at the ball which will end up in the tin. How many times has the overhead volley been crashed into the lower reaches of the tin? And for the simple reason that the stroke is rushed and the racket head has come through too early. The desire is, understandably, to hit the volley vulnerable to attack downwards, but there are limits as to how far down! But if the volley is the stroke where snatching at the ball is most apparent, snatching is itself a weakness that can be applied to any stroke. To overcome that tendency, you should concentrate on rhythm, timing and a carefully paced, controlled swing (see illustration).

Over-cutting
There is natural cutting of the ball on certain shots, backhand drops most particularly. It can also be used on other shots – the attacking volley for example – to make them more decisive, but there is a danger of over-cutting because of the acute timing necessary. When cutting is overdone the racket comes across the face of the ball too severely and the ball finishes up in the tin. An easier but worthwhile alternative, and one that achieves a similar result on shots where cutting is not a natural feature, is to play with a fuller racket face, which will produce the gentle touch you are aiming for.

Addressing the ball incorrectly
You may often have wondered why, when you are attempting to put the ball straight down the wall, it comes back towards you, sometimes hitting you, sometimes just missing you. This is a cause for some concern for, in the context of a match, such an occurrence would mean a stroke awarded against you, but it is easily remedied. Either you played through the ball too early, caused by too quick a stroke, or you opened up the leading shoulder and finished up square-on to the front wall.

In the latter case, it may be that you started off facing the front wall and then lost position, but there are players who consistently address the ball in a position square-on to the front wall. Don't. Think for a moment about the similarities between squash and cricket and it's not difficult to see why good squash players are often good cricketers too. Both games involve a small, fast-moving ball which requires a traditional sideways stance to deal with it, whether with a bat or a racket face. Cricket experts today are frequently to be heard bemoaning the lack of technique of batsmen who adopt an open stance. Adopting a square-on stance to the front wall in squash produces similar technical complications.

It is easy to snatch at the overhead volley or play it too early. The shot requires good positioning, careful watching of the ball and relaxed striking through the ball.

RIGHTING THE WRONGS

The main point about weaknesses is to identify them and then to set about remedying them, recognizing best how this is to be done. Natural talent is enviable, but every player has weaknesses in some area or other. Those with innate athletic and racket ability may be blessed, but instead of bemoaning any shortage in these departments, remember that you can work hard to improve the foundation-stone of the game, which is sound technique, and that those actual qualities you may lack are far less valuable if they are not accompanied in equal measure by mental toughness. So, if you have mental resilience, congratulations – that attribute may be the blessing of all blessings.

A character reference: Abject Failure

Although Mr Abject Failure plays three times a week, albeit against the same opponent, he is badly out of condition, mainly because of the amount of time he spends afterwards in the bar and the business lunches he has most days of the week. His lack of condition is evident in his shape, so he would be well advised, when he does play a fresh opponent, not to change into his kit publicly, and thereby give his opponent's morale a boost! His game is based almost entirely on hacking the ball cross court – mainly anywhere, hoping to disconcert his opponent by the irregularity of it all. Generally he will attempt to hack the ball hard, but as the match progresses he loses power and ends up a pale imitation of the powerful, all-action player he was at the outset.

Abject has never played a drop in his life – nor a lob for that matter – since he regards both as insufficiently macho and dismisses them as 'girls' shots'. These excuses only cover up the fact that he has about as much touch as a blacksmith's hammer and couldn't play a drop if he tried.

He has never watched a match of any quality in his life on the grounds that it would bear no relation to his own game and anyway 'the rallies go on too long'. Besides he is not wholly convinced that these quality players would be able to cope with his all-action game.

He dismisses graphite rackets as new-fangled and much prefers the wooden one which he has had for six years. 'Why change now?' he asks. Nor does he think much of the black ball, preferring, as he says, one with a bit of life in it, referring to the well-tried green fliers he uses regularly. He doesn't think the ball makes much odds to the game and so he believes far too much fuss is made about it.

He has never read the rules, but that doesn't stop him contesting any point where he is of the opinion that his opponent has infringed. Despite his modest standard, Abject is highly competitive and resents any defeat, though he is at the same time a gracious and sporting winner. To get the desired win he will, if necessary, stoop to dubious tactics, such as time-wasting, quick serving, blocking or even physical violence, if the situation is desperate.

Deep down Abject hankers after improvement, but he can't quite bring himself to acknowledge that practice or coaching would be good for him.

THE MIND AT PLAY

THE REQUIREMENTS FOR SUCCESS

If you have deficiencies in your racket skills or physical make-up you can do much to remedy them. Regular, hard practice will certainly bring about improvement with your racket, and physical training will deal with lack of strength – but if you have psychological weaknesses, it is arguable whether these can be righted to the same degree.

These may show up in different ways. You may not be able to 'stick at it'; you may look for excuses for losing, such as arguing with referees (a common escape device!) or you may withdraw from tournaments and even avoid entering them if things are going badly.

What are your best defences against such problems? Probably the best defence is the support and assistance of a coach, although this may not be the complete solution. This is because this type of relationship sadly does not last for ever and when the prop is removed you may be left worse off than you were originally. The greater the bolstering the coach has given you the more likely it is to be missed.

Nothing better illustrates this point than the recent assistance given by Jonah Barrington to David Lloyd. Always vulnerable as a junior player, liable to fail to show at tournaments and sometimes lacking competitive instinct, Lloyd then came under the powerful influence of one of the game's supreme motivators. Lloyd made rapid strides in accordance with the talent that everyone recognized, culminating in splendid performances in the World Junior Championships and success in the British under-23 Open, a world class event. When Jonah moved away and the relationship was more or less dissolved, the old failings manifested themselves, principally in avoidance, so that Lloyd does not play tournaments, especially domestic ones, where his status would be challenged.

The player who faces up to having such problems might do better looking to his own resources. Defence against mental weakness can be found more safely in the knowledge that you have done regular hard work. Add to this a smooth, uncomplicated preparation for any particular tournament or match and some of your fears, at least, should be allayed.

Experience will bring its own rewards: once

you have been through certain situations, you will be better equipped to face them next time (though of course if the situations end up in disaster, the mental problems may be intensified). Physical training is another means of hardening your mental resolve. If you can learn to cope with the demands of hard physical effort you will gather mental strength from this.

One thing is for sure: whatever the differences in the abilities of Geoff Hunt, Jonah Barrington and Jahangir Khan, their mental resolve remains unquestioned. Looking at great performers in other sports, such as Jack Nicklaus, Rod Laver, Steve Cram and Daley Thompson suggests that mental resolve is the most important aspect of an athlete's make up. McEnroe and Connors are less obvious examples of the archetypal world champion, but, though both have their share of temperament, their mental capacity to succeed is hardly in doubt. Do not confuse temperament with lack of mental resolution. Whereas mental weakness may well manifest itself in a show of temperament, temperament itself is not a proof of weakness.

Because of the closeness of the two players on a squash court, any weakness or lack of resolve is easy to detect. In the same way, a player may communicate determination to compete whatever the difficulties. It takes only a little experience to recognize these two situations.

We have all heard, 'He's so talented – if only . . .' What those who make the remark don't appear to appreciate is that it is the other qualities required for success that are rarer.

All the great champions I have heard explaining why they have reached their elevated status make hard work their prime factor. Few, if any, talk about talent; maybe because there is an acceptance that they all have a basic talent and it is how they have applied it that is significant. They all know players who have made a high grade through diligence rather than exceptional talent; they all know performers who could have made the grade if they had added hard work to an obvious natural ability.

Squash, being the demanding game that it

is, requires harder work than most sports, since the high level of racket skill and physical conditioning is not easily come by. There will be times when, as a hard-pressed squash player, you will certainly not feel like working hard, and they will be the testing times. Allied to hard work you will need persistence, which will help you to cope with the ups and downs, the defeats and the disappointments. The same persistence will be required on the court – the ability to fight back when behind, to hang on under pressure and to never let opponents win rallies easily.

Every player will have disappointing losses, will fail at some time or other to win when it is especially important to do so; but there is no point in dwelling on what has happened, unless there is a lesson to be learned. The answer to these disappointments is to get back to work and look for the next immediate opportunity to restore the winning habit and with it, confidence.

Composure is a vital requisite of squash; the pace at which the game is played does not allow for the loss of it. Unlike in most sports, there are no long pauses during the action or between games in which to contemplate what is going wrong. Dwelling on an error, distraction or controversial refereeing decision may well mean a series of mistakes.

It is necessary, too, to be composed so that you can produce shots in a relaxed and controlled manner. If you lose composure you will begin to rush, lose your balance and miss the shot.

In physical terms, squash demands a combination of speed and stamina, allied to physical strength. Stamina does not imply always keeping to the same pace, as this would be of little value. Nor is an excess of speed the answer if you cannot sustain it, so the balance

has to be more or less right and where it is not, you must be prepared to put in some hard work to correct it. If you can get the combination of these two principal physical requirements about right, it should lead to the durability you will need in a hard match and over the course of a long season.

Durability will lead to that other professional virtue – consistency, which will not only earn the respect of potential opponents, but certainly help any professional's earning capacity. For the non-professional, it will mean regular selection.

Everyone who has played a hard squash match will recognize the feeling of wondering whether the pain is worth enduring. In those instances it is the player with the most courage who will survive. It is at these worst moments that some comparisons may be drawn with boxing, though I am by no means suggesting that squash reaches the same extremes. I have noticed, though, that just as in boxing one fight can drain all the resolve from a fighter so that he is never the same again, a series of hard matches can have a telling effect on a squash player.

The most obvious example of this comparison was the gargantuan attempt by that mercurial Egyptian Gamal Awad to beat Jahangir Khan at Chichester in 1983. At that time Awad was one of the very few players who believed he could beat the World No. 1 and, at a time when many leading players were throwing in the towel, he gave it one almighty shot. He played the match of his life and kept Khan on court for 2 hours 46 minutes before finally going down. He has never been the same since. The next time the two men met in competition, Awad was swept aside in 22 minutes.

In research carried out on leading coaches in varying sports, it was found that the most successful concerned themselves not only with every aspect of the game itself, but with their players' backgrounds and how outside factors affect performance. In a game like squash which calls for so much concentration, you cannot play to your best standard if you have too much on your mind. At any level of the game a preoccupied mind will make it

The talented and very promising Rodney Martin (right) plays a backhand angle against Stuart Davenport in the 1987 Telesquash tournament.

IMPROVING YOUR CHANCES

difficult for you to compete, and a professional will find it far from easy to maintain his or her daily routine. It is in this area that a coach should be aware of any problems and be willing to help solve them. If you are in this situation but do not have a coach you will have to learn to deal with them yourself.

It is unrealistic to suppose that squash players will be free from the external problems that beset everyone else, so solving them is essential to doing well. Certainly a stable personal life and day-to-day routine will help any player to perform at his or her best. At the very least, if you are happy at the club where you practise and play, and if practical difficulties such as travelling are kept down to a minimum, it will give you a sound basis on which to flourish.

There is a school of thought which believes that deprivation is the source from which champions are made, and although it may well not stop someone determined to reach the top – certainly true in boxing – on balance good facilities and support seem to me a more likely background. It is hard enough to make the grade; deprivation may well make it impossible. But do not let plenty of opportunities mislead you; the route to the top in any sport is not easy.

One of the advantages of competing at the highest levels is that it generally helps players to keep a sense of perspective about themselves. Those who aspire to the top know there are always some who are better. It would have been difficult in the last five years for any world-class player to have had too high an opinion of himself since he would know that he was not in the same class as Jahangir Khan. It is not my experience that world class players have themselves out of proportion. They are too aware of their own shortcomings. Modesty becomes any top class performer.

Squash has been very well served in this important respect by the most recent of its great champions: Jonah Barrington, Geoff Hunt, Jahangir Khan, the great Heather McKay and the current leading lady, Susan Devoy.

A sense of humour too has never done anyone much harm and while I am not a subscriber to the 'it's only a game' school of thought, life is arguably only a game. The ability not to take a sport too seriously will be a help, particularly at the low times. If you are aiming for the top, a sense of humour will make the daily working routine more acceptable as will working with partners whose outlook is similar to your own. And even if you're not, anything that helps you to enjoy the sport will be to your advantage, for it is the love of the game and the enjoyment you derive from it that will keep you going – and, indeed, is the reason for playing.

A sound mental approach, together with talent and physical fitness, supported by the abstract qualities I have mentioned, will make for a well rounded player. No-one will have all the qualities in full; some players will be strong in some areas, less so in others. The imbalances will need working on, so that they don't show as weaknesses. It is not easy to put the various qualities necessary for success in order of importance, as the competition makers would have us do but, all things considered, mental strength is undoubtedly the one requisite that the ambitious player must not lack.

PERSPECTIVES

Ross Norman on ending Jahangir Khan's 5½ year undefeated run in the 1986 World Open final in Toulouse:

"I won as I always thought I would. I always said it would take 2½ hours to wear him down. I knew that one day he would be off his game and I would be playing well and I would get him.

"It was an amazing feeling. At last I could let go and just shout for joy. I had done it the hard way, worn him off the court, the greatest player this game has seen."

Jahangir Khan on losing his world crown and his unbeaten record:

"It had to happen some time. I have done everything else in the game. Now I have the chance for a comeback at 22 years of age."

Hiddy Jahan and Lars Kvant show that winning isn't everything; 1984 World Masters tournament.

LEARNING BY WATCHING

WHAT TO LOOK FOR

Apart from being properly taught at an early stage – a benefit that many squash players may not have enjoyed – one of the ways in which players may learn is by watching those more accomplished than themselves. Many times, after having watched the world's best players in action at major championships, I have, on returning home, played very well by my standards, though I have to admit for a relatively short time! For a younger, more impressionable player the benefits from watching are likely to last much longer, even to the extent of becoming part of his or her game. It is important, therefore, that you know how to watch, what to watch and which players to watch and to be influenced by.

There may well be advantages in watching the best players in the local club if they are of the right sort; there are tournaments held in all parts of the country where there are sure to be some higher standard players worth watching. And, of course, there are major championships such as the British Closed and Open, where the best players in the world can be seen in action.

It is worth looking at the qualities of some of the foremost names in squash, isolating their particular strengths, so that if you have the opportunity to see them in action, you will be aware of specific aspects of their game to look out for.

Most of the players under scrutiny are still on the international scene, even if some of them are playing in over-35 and over-45 events, which have the splendid advantage of giving everybody the chance to watch the world's great players of yesteryear. They are no less watchable for being older and moving less spectacularly than they did during their heyday, and, indeed, some of them play still to remarkably high standards.

An examination of the qualities of world class players, necessarily brief, will doubtless produce recurring characteristics, but a consideration of all the players proves above all how individual they are.

It is remarkable how squash seems to throw up truly outstanding world champions, who seem, in a highly competitive and demanding game, to rise consistently above the standards of the nearest challengers. The current two leading players, Jahangir Khan and Susan Devoy, certainly fall into that category.

Susan Devoy is an extraordinary champion, combining technical excellence with mental and physical extreme toughness. She is quick to attack at the first opportunity and yet her game has a balanced, secure look about it. Above all her other technical attributes, she plays beautifully down the backhand side, notable being her drops from both the front of the court and the back.

One of her main challengers over recent years has been, and still is, Lisa Opie, who has a range and variety of shot as good as any player in the game, man or woman. Lisa, like Susan, is especially strong down the backhand side and one shot I always associate with her is the cross court lob off the volley, mostly on the backhand side, a very difficult proposition.

Vicky Caldwell and Rhonda Thorne, two leading women players of just a few years ago, both Australians, but who are less in evidence on the world scene nowadays, had quite different attributes: Vicky being the essential competitor; while Rhonda was all neatness and quality.

But the greatest woman player of all time was undoubtedly Heather McKay, now involved with Geoff Hunt in running the Australian Institute of Squash. Unbeaten for many years, her hallmark was the consistency of her play and her performances. Her game always looked reliable and dependable, so there was little chance of it ever breaking down, especially as she was as mentally tough as all outstanding world champions have to be.

To move from one outstanding world champion to another, Geoff Hunt, apart from his playing record, was an ambassador par excellence for the sport, on and off the court. He combined on court wondrous movement and athleticism with the same reliability that Heather McKay possessed. In his late playing days, troubled with a back injury, he lost some matches which normally would have been no trouble to him, but he never made an excuse, not even an explanation, and it was only later that his injuries were revealed.

Qamar Zaman, one of Hunt's principal adversaries, has been one of the game's most gifted strokemakers and, luckily, he is still to be seen displaying his skills. Zaman, with his sense of adventure and racket skill to match, is a constant reminder to all squash players everywhere that the game is not just a matter of physical attrition, and for that we all owe him.

Still going strong is another player of the same era, Hiddy Jahan. The way in which he has retained his form and enthusiasm is testimony enough to this great striker of the ball. No player hits the ball with the same consistent ferocity as this powerful Pakistani; but having said that, it would be wrong to suggest that his whole game revolved round force, since there is much more to Hiddy Jahan's game than that.

The delightful Ahmed Safwat, for years the leading Egyptian, still graces the international scene occasionally in over-35 events and what pleasure he gives with his languid, relaxed style on the court and his affability off. Few players, if any, play the angles as well as Ahmed Safwat.

One of the advantages of over-45 tournaments at world level has been that Ken Hiscoe, that notable Australian of the early professional days, has been in evidence. With the same characteristic competitive instinct that he had as a younger man, looking fit and strong, Hiscoe is one of those veteran players who look none the worse for passing years.

Three English 'amateurs' with varying abilities, who are still playing, but who were prominent at high levels until quite recently are worth a mention – Johnny Leslie, Stuart Courtney and Peter Verow.

Of the three, Courtney was the artist with the racket, full of touch and invention, Leslie was the natural athlete, tough and determined, and Verow was the ultimate competitor. All three, if they had been intent on a squash playing career, would have been successful professionals. As it was they had other professions to follow, but they still achieved a great deal.

Gamal Awad, the likeable and diminutive Egyptian, is certainly one of the quickest movers the game has ever seen. Having risen to the top five in the world, he has found difficulty in holding such an exalted position, though he still plays the circuit. At his athletic best he was one of the most entertaining players imaginable.

One of the most exciting young players on the world circuit is the enigmatic Tristan Nancarrow. Consistency is not his trademark, but when he is firing, his cat-like movement and imagination are quite remarkable, thus his ability to pull off surprise and extraordinary wins. There is always room in sport for this type of player, just to remind everyone of the possibilities.

Fellow Australian Chris Dittmar is a left hander of real class. He is worth watching for the disguise in his play, apart from the fact that he moves so well for such a big man. Chris was injured while playing Australian Rules football which set him back in the world rankings for a while, but is now well on his way back to top form.

The current crop of world class players provide interesting contrasts: the athleticism and strength of New Zealand's Ross Norman, winner of the World Championship in Toulouse; the striking power of Norman's compatriot Stuart Davenport; the racket skills of Gawain Briars when he is in harmony with the game; the all-round competence of the affable Ross Thorne.

Add together all the qualities of these many exceptional players and the one man currently who has most of them is the world's foremost player, Jahangir Khan. Unbeaten for five

Bryan Beeson and Mark Maclean, two players whose stars are in the ascendant.

WATER TORTURE

"I love this game for its deep, individual competitiveness and its wonderful comradeship. I played team squash for Elm Club in Melbourne where we used to have a cold water award in the shower room for the worst performance of the night. When I lost the 1970 British Open final to Jonah Barrington, my old Elm Club teammates sent me a message by special delivery. Not sympathy or commiserations, just a bucket of cold water." – *Geoff Hunt, the first official world champion and 8 times winner of the British Open*

Mohamed Yasin and Ken Hiscoe in the hard-fought 1985 British Open veterans' final, showing that the years had not diminished their appetite for the game. Yasin went on to win and so deny Hiscoe his hat-trick in this event. Hiscoe got his revenge in the 1986 final.

and a half years, until the World Championship at Toulouse in November 1986, looking for flaws in his game is harder than looking for a needle in a haystack.

It is because he has so few weaknesses that he has been able to remain unbeaten for so long. He has the composure of an outstanding champion and preserves the balance of defence and attack which best serves his winning ways.

No player has contributed more to the development and advancement of the game than arguably its most notable personality, Jonah Barrington. Through his achievements and involvement with the sport, squash became a liberated game instead of one bounded by gentlemen's clubs, officers' messes and public schools.

Still practising with the verve and enthusiasm of youth, still producing fine performances at the top over-35 and over-45 levels, Jonah Barrington has a charisma, special to only a few. To see him in action is to see one of the sport's greatest figures.

Every one of the players I have mentioned is worth watching for one reason or another and there are many others with similar admirable qualities. So, my advice would be to use discriminate watching of the best players to learn how to play better and improve your game. High class squash is relatively accessible in this country, and anyone who is eager to improve but does not take such an opportunity is missing out.

AFTERTHOUGHTS

Having coached rugby and cricket as well as squash for many years, I became increasingly involved with squash as the game developed until finally my involvement was total. Gone are the chilly May days in the nets, and the cold and rain of English winters. Much though cricket and rugby have to offer, I have not the slightest regret that my time and energy are given to squash.

To be concerned from the beginning with any game that has developed as spectacularly as squash is an adventure, and a privilege. The game has so much to offer: it provides socially based exercise for those without too serious intent, and for those more competitively inclined it is a thorough test of physical and mental capacity. It fits into the pattern of modern life, not needing to occupy too much time, and it is hardly affected by a capricious climate.

What still surprises me after 37 years in the sport is that I am still learning, yet to look at the bare confines of the squash court, it would appear that the game would have to be simple and limited in its scope. It's not – as readers of this book will discover, if they haven't already! So, keep playing and keep learning!

It would be an impossible task to thank individually all those who have influenced and helped my work in squash, and so contributed to the contents of this book. Much that has shaped my coaching philosophy has been learned from coaches in other sports.

My thanks to all those notable and famous players and personalities for providing apt and interesting quotes for the book; to Jonah Barrington for his foreword and for the inspiration he provides just in talking to him; and, finally, to Lesley, my wife, for supporting an irregular lifestyle for the sake of the game I love, though not quite as much as her!

Malcolm Willstrop

Page numbers in *italic* refer to illustrations

addressing the ball, correcting faults, 64-5
advice from the sidelines, 59
aims of squash, *55*
Alauddin, Gogi, 16
angles, 15-18, *15-18*
    practice games, 43
    practicing, 28, 29; 32-3, *32-3*
    return of serve, 21
arrival time, match preparation, 49
Awad, Gamal, 67, 73
awareness, 52

backhand angles, *16*
backhand drops, 23, *23*
backhand lob, *25*
backhand serves, 20
balance, correcting faults, 60
Barrington, Jonah, *7*, 44, 66, 77
Beeson, Bryan, *9*, 38, *50-1, 75*
blind spots, 61
boast, 15
Bodimeade, Martin, *41*
Briars, Gawain, 46, *60*, 73
British Doubles Championships, 1986, 41
British Open, 1985, *77*

Caldwell, Vicky, 72
Carter, Paul, *41*
co-operative volleying, 33-4, *34*
coaches, 59, 66
composure, 63-4, 67
condition games, 41-3
    above the cut line, 42
    angles across the court, 42
    angles only, 42
    behind the mid court line, 42
    below the cut line, 42
    continuous squash, 43
    lob and drop, 43
    playing the ball into either rectangle, 43
    returning the serve straight, 42-3
    straight v normal, 41-2
consistency, 67
Cornish, Jon, *41*
court conditions, 52
court craft, 52-9
    advice from the sidelines, 59
    aims, *55*
    changing pace, 56-7
    court conditions, 52
    flexibility, 57-8
    improvisation, 58-9

opening moves, 52-6
    play in progress, 52
    shot selection, 56
Courtney, Stuart, 73
Cowie, Alex, 36, *59*
cross court drop, 24
cross court hitting, 12-14, *28*
    practice, 28
cross court lob, 25
    practising, 28-9
cross court nicks, *27*, 34-5

Davenport, Stuart, *69*, 73
deep angles, 21
defensive angle, 16
Devoy, Susan, 23, *25*, 72
Dittmar, Chris, *1*, 73
double feeds, 35, *35*
doubles, practice games, 43
drops:
    practice games, 43
    practicing, 30-2, *31*, 32-3
durability, 67

eating, match preparation, 48
equipment, match preparation, 48
exercises, 44-7
    movement on court, 45
    running, 44-5
    stretching, 45-7
    weight training, 44

faults, 60-5
    addressing the ball, 64-5
    balance, 60
    blind spots, 61
    composure, 63-4
    footwork, 60-1
    keeping feet still, 60-1
    overcutting, 64
    overrunning the ball, 61
    racket control, 61-3
    running directly at the ball, 61
feeding:
    double, 35-7, *35, 36*
    practice, 26
final practice, match preparation, 48
fitness, training, 44-7
flexibility, 57-8
floater, 25
footwork, correcting faults, 60-1
forehand angles, *15, 16*, 18, *18*
forehand volleys, *13*
front court game, 40-1

games, practice, 38-43
Gibson, Mike, 59

green balls, drop shot and, 22
grip, 10
group practice, 38

Harris, Del, 59
Hickox, Jamie, 59
high volleys, 14
Hiscoe, Ken, 73, *77*
Hunt, Georff, 16, 44, 66, 72, 77

improving your game, 8-9
improvisation, 58-9
Irving, Liz, 14

Jahan, Hiddy, 30, *71*, 73
James, Carwyn, 59

keeping feet still, 60-1
keeping fresh, match preparation, 49
Kenyon, Phil, 11
Khan, Jahangir, 14, 44, *47*, 66, 67, 70, 73-7
knocking up, match preparation, 49
Kvant, Lars, *71*

Leslie, Johnny, 73
Lloyd, David, 66
lobs, 24-5, *24, 25*, 28
    practice games, 43
    practicing, 28-9, 32
looking at squash, 72-7
low shots, 12
low volleys, 14

Mabbs, Darren, *41*
McKay, Heather, 72
Maclean, Mark, 44, *75*
McQuillan, Colin, 49
Martin, Rodney, *69*
match preparation, 48-51
    eating, 48
    equipment, 48
    final practice, 48
    keeping fresh, 49
    knocking up, 49-51
    preliminaries, 48
    team responsibilities, 49
    timing your arrival, 48-9
    warming up, 49
mental approach, 66-71
    requirements for success, 66-7
    will to win, 67
movement on court, 45

Nancarrow, Tristan, 27, 73
Naylor, Ashley, *50-1*
nicks, cross court, *27*, 34-5
Norman, Ross, *62*, 70, 73

one for the volley, 40
one versus two, 38
opening moves, 52-6
Opie, Lisa, *39*, 72
overcutting, 64
overrunning the ball, 61

pace, changing, 56-7
Pearson, David, *56*
physical training, 44-7
playing conditions, 52
playing down the walls, 38
practice, 8, 26
    feeding, 26
    group, 38
    routines, 26
    shots, 26-37
    solo, 37, *37*
    straight hitting, 26
practice games, 38-43
    above the cut line, 42
    angles across the court, 42
    angles only, 42
    behind the mid court line, 42
    below the cut line, 42
    condition games, 41-3
    continuous squash, 43
    doubles, 43
    front court game, 40-1
    lob and drop, 43
    one versus two, 38
    one for the volley, 40
    playing the ball into either rectangle, 43
    playing down the walls, 38
    returning the serve straight, 42-3
    straight v normal, 41-2
    three ball, 38
preliminaries, match preparation, 48
psychological approach, 66-71
    requirements for success, 66-7
    will to win, 67

racket control, 61-2
    correcting faults, 61-3
    dropping the wrist, 62
    follow through, 62
    preparation, 62
racket, grip, 10
receiving service, 21-2, *21*
reverse angle, *18*
Robinson, Ian, 35
running:

INDEX

directly at the ball, 61
training, 44-5

Safwat, Ahmed, 16, *17*, 73
Saunders, Doug, 63
sense of humour, 70
service, 18-20, *19, 20, 55*
  backhand, 20
  return of, 21-2, *21*
Shawcross, Kevin, 73
short angles, 16, *16*, 18
shots:
  angles, 15-18, *15-18*, 28, 29, 32-3, *32, 33*
  boast, 15
  cross court hitting, 12-14, 28, *28*
  drops, 22-4, *22-4*, 30-3, *31*
  lobs, 24-5, *24, 25*, 28, 32
  overcutting, 64

practicing, 26-37
return of service, 21-2, *21*
selection, 56
service, 18-20, *19, 20*
straight hitting, 10-12, *10*, 26-8
volleys, *13*, 14-15, *14*
solo practice, 37, *37*
Soutter, Lucy, *57*, 67
stamina, 67
Stevenson, David, 61
straight hitting, 10-12, *10*
  practice routines, 26-7
stretching exercises, 45-7

tactics, 52-9
  advice from the sidelines, 59
  aims, *55*
  changing pace, 56-7
  court conditions, 52

flexibility, 57-8
improvisation, 58-9
opening moves, 52-6
play in progress, 52
shot selection, 56
team responsibilities, match
  preparation, 49
Telesquash, 1987, *50-1, 69*
Thorne, Rhonda, 72
Thorne, Ross, 19, *60*, 73
three ball, 38
training, 44-7
  movement on court, 45
  running, 44-5
  stretching, 45-7
  weight training, 44
  see also practice
two angles, *32*, 33, *33*

Verow, Peter, 73

volley drops, 32
volleys, *13*, 14-15, *14*
  angles, 28-9
  co-operative, 33-4, *34*
  practice, 28
  return of serve, 21
  rushing, 64
  solo practice, 37

watching squash, 72-7
weight training, 44
Williams, Dean, 48
Willstrop, Christy, 42
World Masters, 1984, *71*

Yasin, Mohamed, *77*

Zaman, Qamar, *53*, 73